# The Green & Tree

## Damh The Bard Songbook 1

by Damh The Bard

www.capallbann.co.uk

# The Green & Burning Tree



ISBN 186163 333 5
ISBN 13 978186163 333 0



First published in England in 2007 by Caer Bryn Music


Cover design by HR Design
www.hr-design.co.uk
Photographs by Richard Paris

Published by:

Capall Bann Publishing
Auton Farm
Milverton
Somerset
TA4 1NE

## Dedication

'Dedicated to my parents, to my partner Cerri, to my sons Zach and Josh, and to every musical traveller who seeks the Otherworld within the Green.'

My parents - 1982

# Introduction

I started writing these songs in 1997 and I must admit I never thought I would ever be asked to produce a song book, but as time passed, more and more people have asked me to produce one.

The mere thought of it filled me with dread – for someone who cannot read music, I tend to steer clear of song books as they are of little use to me. I tried to find someone who could set the notation professionally, but the cost was too prohibitive..... and the requests kept coming, and I kept promising. So, in the end I have made a few compromises so that I can get this to you.

There are no musical staves for the vocal line – I'm hoping that you didn't just buy this book, and that you have the recordings of the songs, so you can sing along and get a feel of the vocal melody. The other compromise is that I tend to make up a lot of my chords. Now I know that they must have proper names, but I've chosen to go down a 'creative' route, by giving some of the more unusual chords names such as AI, BII and CSI etc. I'm sure that there'll be purists out there who are shaking in horror at the thought of such heresy, but my main aim was to produce a song book that was useable for people, and this is the result. I guess this strange format might give a bit of insight into my song writing method, ie, if it sounds good and suits the song, it must be a chord...

Occasionally a song was written on the mandolin, mandola, or bouzouki, and in a couple of cases, I've included the original chords from that instrument.

What an adventure! I hope you enjoy playing these songs around campfires, in your Groves and Covens, at festivals, and just by yourself.

Peace, and blessed be,
Damh

# Contents

# Song of Awen

## (Damh the Bard)

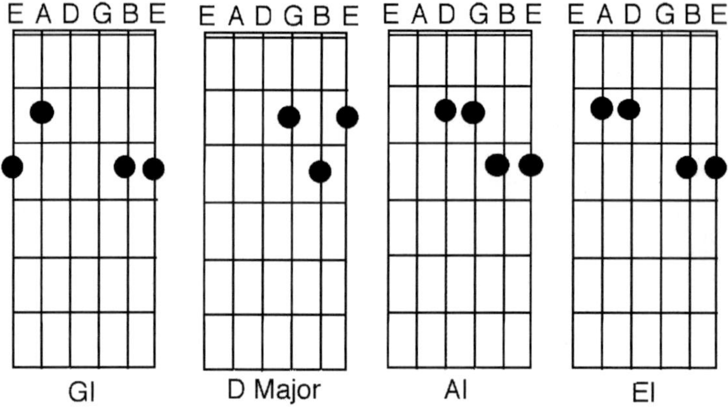


Awen is the 'flowing spirit' of Bardic inspiration and creativity. I wanted to write a song that summed up how I felt about the beauty, and wonder, of the natural world. A song that filled me up every time I heard the lyrics, as it told of how the Gods show themselves to us every day through the world of nature. Song of Awen was the result.

Instrument: guitar. Tuning: EADGBE

D               AI
See me as the Sun on the mountaintop,
EI                 GI    AI       D    AI     EI    GI    AI
Feel me in the power    of the seas.
D                AI
Hear me in the laughter of the stream,
EI          GI     AI             D    AI     EI    GI
Power of nature, power of the trees.

**Bridge:**
EI                   GI
It is you who are broken,
EI                 D
You are part of me,

EI                    GI
Some of you have awoken,
EI                             AI
But others might never be free.

**Chorus:**
D                  AI
This is my song, this is my voice,
EI                     GI         AI
These are my words, this is my choice.
D               AI
Hear me now, take heed of my words.
EI               GI            AI         D    AI    EI    GI    AI
Love me now,      and your spirit will fly.

Hear me in the howling of the wolf,
My voice is the song of the Bards,
I am the power that helps the salmon leap,
I am the very first breath of a child.

I am the wild, and I am the tame,
I am the calm and I am the storm.
I am the sound of your beating heart,
I am your blood and I am your bone.

**Bridge 2:**
It is you who are broken,
You are part of me,
There is no separation,
So dance, sing and be free.

# Obsession

(Damh the Bard)

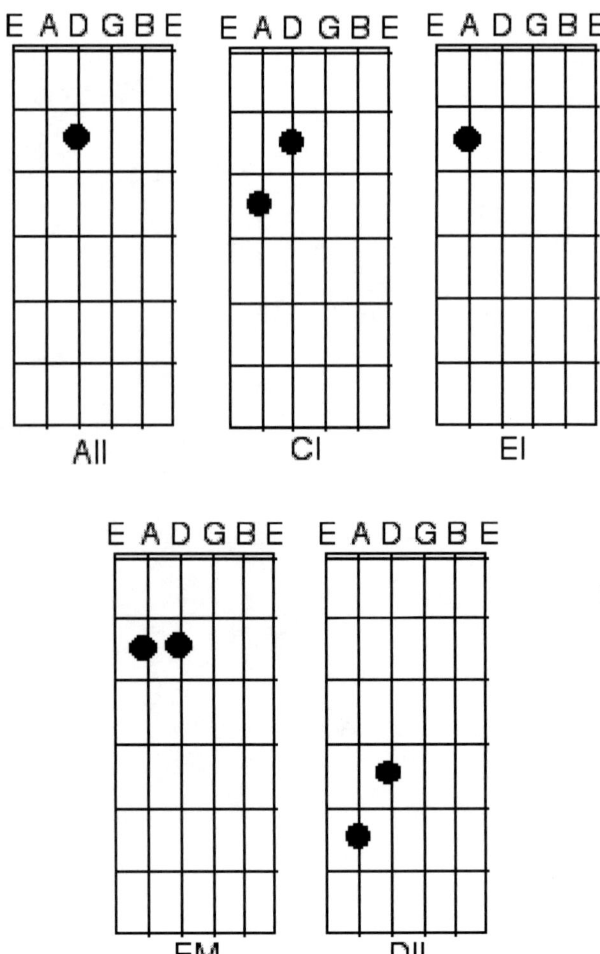

......so I tried to write a love song...... I love singing this song, especially around a camp fire, and smile as the couples get more intimate.....

Instrument: guitar. Tuning: EADGBE (Finger picked)

```
AII                 CI                EI           AII
I am temptation,    and I am the air that you breathe.
AII                     CI           EI          EM
Mine are the lips, and yours is the skin that I tease.
CI                          DII                    AII
When you close your eyes, I am the face that you see.
CI                     DII                    AII
Mine is the voice inviting you to lie with me.
```

I am the vampire at your door, please let me in,
I am the fire that draws the sweat from your skin.
Tooth and nail bring the bitter sweetness of pain.
Your love I drink like the blood that flows in your veins.

Let me come to you and be ther Sun in your sky,
Under my heat on golden corn you will lie,
The Moon may shine but you are the Goddess I see,
And lying there naked you wake up the God within me.

# Blodeuwedd

## (Damh the Bard)

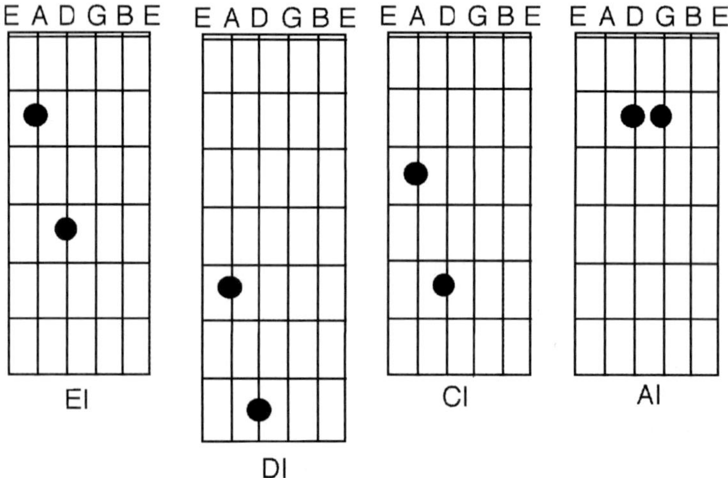


Blodeuwedd is the great Goddess from the fourth branch of the Welsh Mabinogion. This is the second part of a trilogy of songs started with 'Oak Broom and Meadowsweet' and ended with 'Cloak of Feathers'. To many Blodeuwedd is seen as a betrayer, but not to me. She was conjured by Gwydion and Math to be a wife for Lleu Llaw Gyffess, so she was a trapped woman, and we all know that this is NOT a good idea....

Instrument: guitar. Tuning: EADGBE (Finger picked)

EI CI EI CI
Look into the water, tell me what do you see?
EI CI DI CI
I see a woman of flowers crying out to be free.
EI CI EI CI
I see a Goddess, a woman, in a circle of trees.
EI CI DI CI
I see Math and Gwydion fall to their knees.
DI CI
Fall to their knees.

**Chorus:**
AI EI
Welcome the May Queen,
AI EI
Sing for her now,
AI EI
For as the year turns to Samhain
CI DI
She'll return as an owl,
CI DI EI CI DI EI CI DI
Blodeuwedd the owl.

Stand alone in the tower, watch over your land.
Hear the call of a hunter, call him into your hands.
He is dark, he is handsome, and the King is away,
Gronw says he must go now, but you ask him to stay,
Ask him to stay.

She can't live without him, so while the King is away,
They plot to kill him in a year and a day.
With a foot on a cauldron, a goat holds him true.
By a fast running river, came the spear from Gronw,
And the eagle it flew.

My son where are you? For only I see,
An old rotting eagle upon an oak tree.
Come to me young lion and rest this night,
For your wife is a bird now, she will never see light,
Cursed to hunt in the night.

Me, 1 year old

# Fíth Fath Song

## (traditional arr. Damh the Bard)

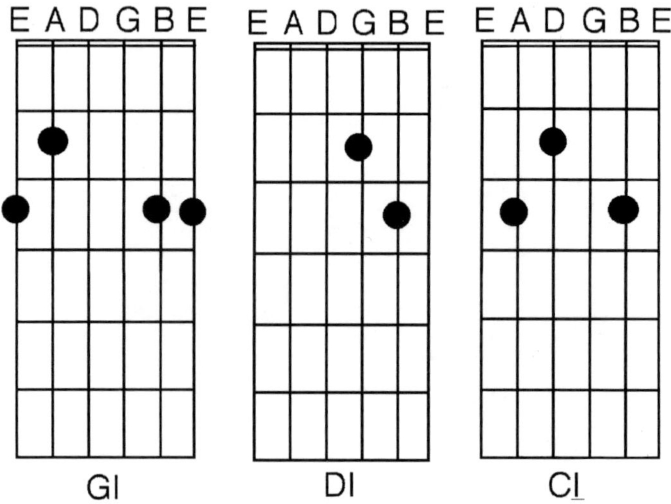


This shape-shifting song, that originates from Scotland, is traditionally sung as part of a Beltane love chase.

Instrument: guitar. Tuning: EADGBE

DI CI DI
I shall go as a wren in Spring,
DI CI DI
With sorrow and sighing on silent wing,
DI CI GI
I shall go in our Lady's name,
DI CI DI
Aye till I come home again.

Then we shall follow as falcons grey,
And hunt thee cruelly for our prey,
And we shall go in our Horned God's name,
Aye to fetch thee home again.

Then I shall go as a mouse in May,
Through fields by night, and in cellars by day,
And I shall go in our Lady's name,
Aye till I come home again.

Then we shall follow as black tom cats,
And hunt thee through the fields and the vats,
And we shall go in our Horned God's name,
Aye to fetch thee home again.

Then I shall go as an Autumn hare,
With sorrow and sighing and mickle care,
And I shall go in our Lady's name,
Aye till I come home again.

Then we shall follow as swift greyhounds,
And dog thy steps with leaps and bounds,
And we shall go in our Horned God's name,
Aye to fetch thee home again.

Then I shall go as a Winter trout,
With sorrow and sighing and mickle doubt,
And I shall go in our Lady's name,
Aye till I come home again.

Then we shall follow as otters swift,
And bind thee fast so thou cans't shift,
And we shall go in our Horned God's name,
Aye to fetch thee home again.

# Cloak of Feathers

## (Damh the Bard)

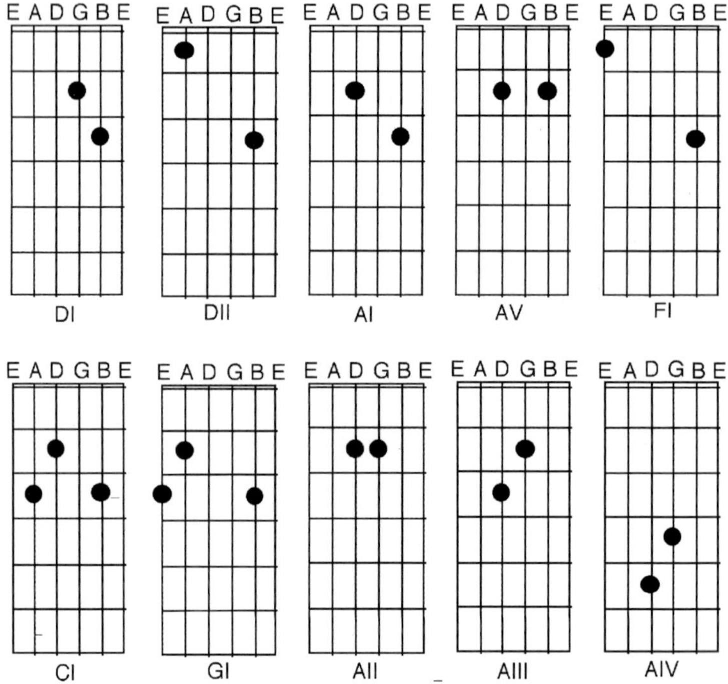


This is the final part of the Blodeuwedd trilogy of songs. When I first began to write Pagan songs I was always aware of a spirit whispering words to me from another place. This spirit was Blodeuwedd, my muse. This song tells of how Blodeuwedd visits a mortal human, and how his love set her free from the curse set upon her by Gwydion, the enchanter.

Instrument: guitar. Tuning: EADGBE

DI CI DI CI
Owl at my window,
DI CI DI CI
Calling from the tree,
DI CI DII AI
I hear our voice in the cool moonlight,
GI FI DI CI DI CI
Do you sing those words for me?

DI CI DI CI
To me they sound so empty,
DI CI DI CI
Why do you sound so sad?
DI CI DII AI
As you tell me of the things you've seen,
GI FI AI AV AI AV
And the home that you once had. home that you once had

**(Chorus 1)**
DI CI GI
Beyond the mist of myth and legend
DI
In a place not far from here,
CI GI
Beneath the stones on the hill,
DI
I want to see you land,
CI GI AI AV
And I wonder if I'll ever, understand.

The owl she told me,
Of her home within the hill.
Of the wonder, and the magic land,
That lies within there still.
But a curse it follows lifetimes,
And it took away her skin,
For the words of a wicked man,
Made birds of her kin.

Owl of the nighttime,
Owl of the sky.
Spread now your ghost-white wings,
And on your back I'll fly.
Over the forest,
To the Hollow Hill of Stones,
Land there within the ring,
And call for your home.

**(Chorus 2)**

Beyond the mist of myth and legend
In a place not far from here,
Beneath the stones on the hill,
I want to see you home,
Give me a Cloak of Feathers so I'll never be alone.
AII AII
And the mists they part as through we fly,
AIV
In my Cloak of Feathers,
AII
The owl and I.
AII
Birds fill the trees in this wonderland,

AIV
And an ancient curse is broken,
AII
By the love of a mortal man.

# Raggle Taggle Gypsies
## (Traditional arr. Damh the Bard)

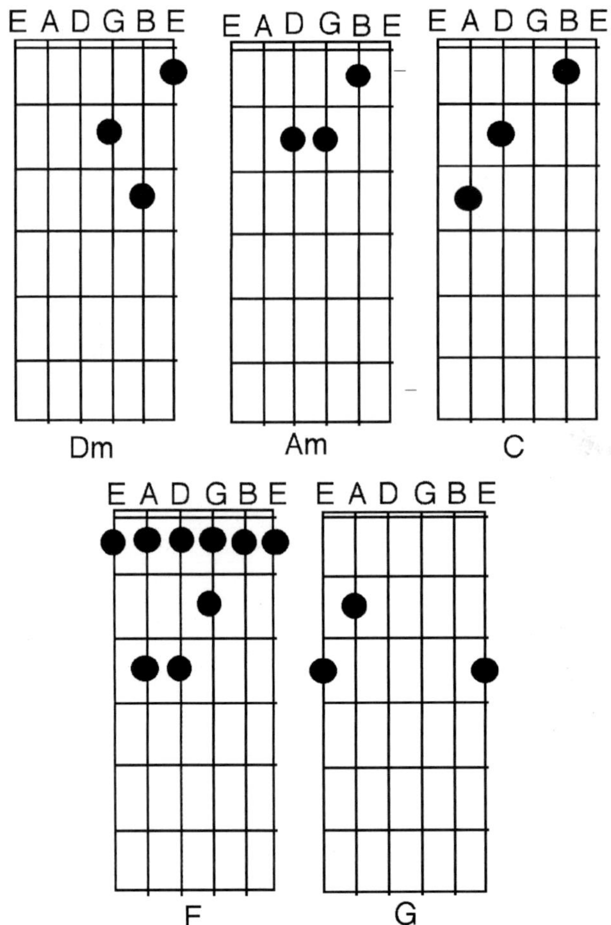

Instrument: guitar. Tuning: EADGBE

```
Dm
There were three young gypsies come to our hall door,
                                   Am
They came brave and boldly-o
      C                           Dm
And one sang high and the other sang low,
          F                  G                Dm
And the other sang the Raggle Taggle Gypsy-o
```

Well it was upstairs downstairs the lady went
Put on her suit of leather-o
And there was a cry from around the door,
She's away with the Raggle Taggle Gypsy-o

It was late that night when the Lord came in,
Enquiring for his Lady-o
And the servant girl she said to the Lord,
She's away with the Raggle Taggle Gypsy-o

Then saddle for me my milk-white steed,
My big horse is not speedy-o,
Tonight I'll ride, to seek my bride,
She's away with the Raggle Taggle Gypsy-o

Well he rode east, and he rode west,
He rode north and south also,
Until he came to a wide open plane,
That's where he spied his Lady-o.

How could you leave your house and your land?
How could you leave your money-o?
How could you leave your newly-wedded Lord,
All for the Raggle Taggle Gypsy-o?

Well what care I for my house and my land?
What do I care for money-o?
I'd rather have a kiss from a yellow gypsy's lips,
I'm away with the Raggle Taggle Gypsy-o

How could you leave your house and your land?
How could you leave your money-o?
How could you leave your newly-wedded Lord,
All for the Raggle Taggle Gypsy-o?

Well what care I for my house and my land?
What do I care for money-o?
Tonight I'll lie in a wide open field,
In the arms of my Raggle Taggle Gypsy-o

# Lughnasadh
## (Damh the Bard)

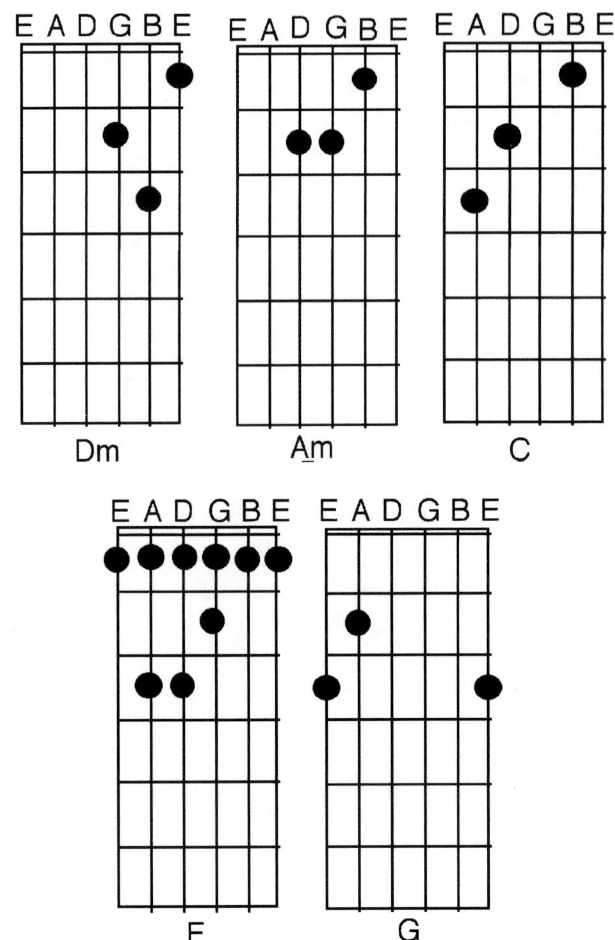

I really wanted to write a 'foot-stomper' for old John Barleycorn. So this song tells the story of the Corn King, from birth, to death, to rebirth.

Instrument: Guitar. Tuning EADGBE

Dm C G Dm
Feel me sleep beneath your feet
C G Dm
While the year is waning,
C G Dm
And all about you the bare fingers plead
C G Dm
And reach towards the sky,
C G Dm
A crown of thorns about my head,
C G Dm
When the dark is rising,
C G Dm
And from the shadows walks a God, a seed,
C G Dm
A hope for brand new life.

**(Bridge)**
Dm
Can you hear the Spirits of the Earth can you?
F
Can you hear the Spirits of the Earth can you?
Am
Can you hear the Spirits of the Earth?
C G
Can you hear them call, can you hear them sing

**(Chorus)**

```
Dm              C                         G
Lughnasadh! Is the life and the death of the Corn King,
Dm              F                                   Dm
Lughnasadh! Life and rebirth of the Corn King!
Dm              C                         G
Lughnasadh! Is the life and the death of the Corn King,
Dm              F                                  Dm
Lughnasadh! Life and rebirth of the Corn King!
```

I turn my green face to the Sun,
As the year is waxing,
And all about animals call my name
In forest and in sky.
My horns of velvet reflect the Moon,
Silver wheel of my Lady,
She comes towards me as the May reveals
Her White and virgin skin.

I turn my gold face to the Sun
As the year is waning,
The time has come now for my life to end
As metal rubs on stone,
She comes towards me across the fields,
Chariot's wheels a-blazing,
Her hair on fire, cut me crush me, bake me,
Eat me, I am yours

Me on my rocking horse - where I learnt to sing

# The Pipes of Pan
## (Damh the Bard)

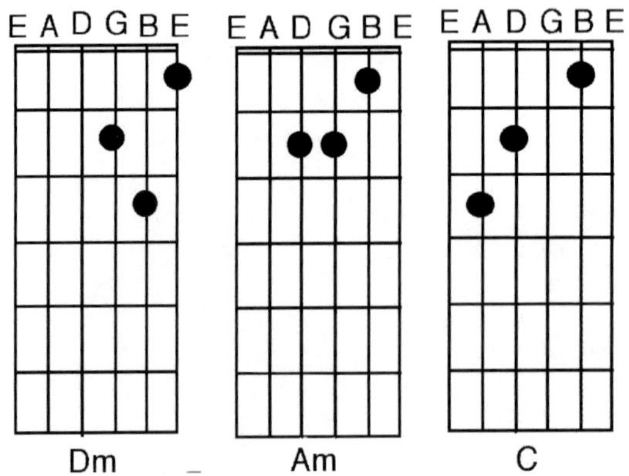


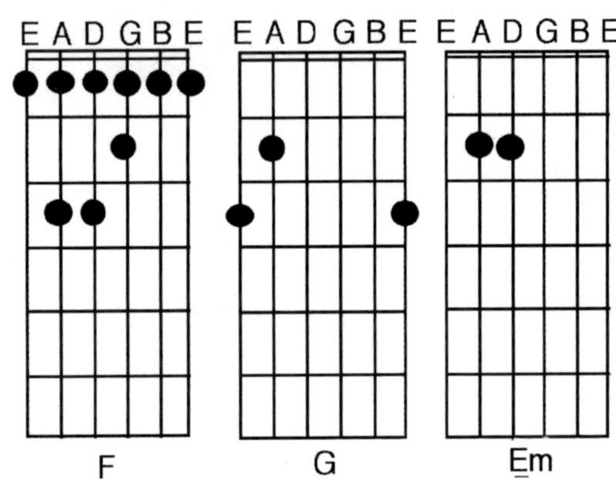

The idea for this song came about while I was driving across Dartmoor, and having to quickly avoid some of the local drivers. I began to wonder how long you had to live in a place before you stopped seeing the beauty that surrounded you. Before the journey stopped mattering, and the arrival was all that existed...

Instrument: guitar. Tuning: EADGBE

C                              Am
Can you hear the distant thunder?
C                          Em
Can you see the Moon in the sky?
C                  Am              C
I can see a full horizon,      the Sun raising his eye.
Am                 Em
Arms lifted to greet the dawn,
    F                             Am
As fiery eyes of wisdom shine,
Dm                     Em
A father dead, a Son of Suns,
          F                         G
A tear wiped away with a smile.

**(Chorus)**
C                                 Am                       Em
All of my life I have seen many offerings,
           F                          G                           C
To the Gods and all the wonder that they hold.
                                            Am                                Em
But how many people really can, hear the pipes of Pan?
            F                           G                  C
As they sound across our sacred land of old

I can see a cloven hoof falling,
On the bare skin of the Earth.
I can see life returning, feel the triple One's rebirth.
Golden light dapples across the woodland,
As the Piper dances and plays his tune.
Herne the Hunter, Horned One,
Spirit of Man to the Moon.

Can you hear the pipes of Pan
On the warm Summer breeze?
If you can, can you feel him deep within you
As he penetrates the land?
May blossom to the bee,
The nectar of love is on her skin.
Heat returns as passions rise
And Beltane's dance begins, once again.

# Learning to Fly
## (Damh the Bard)

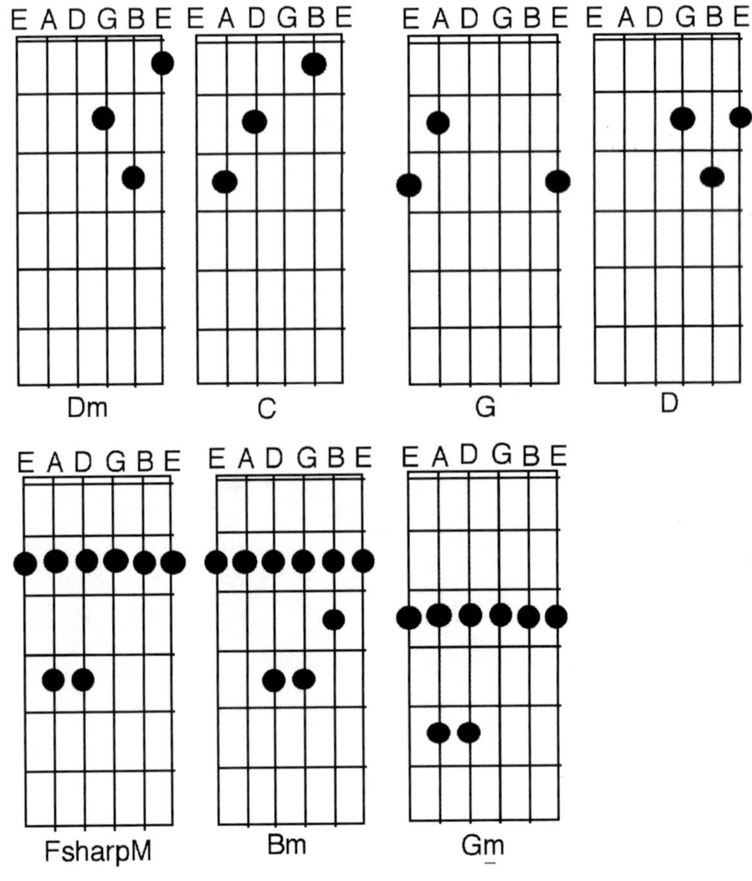

I wrote this song doing exactly as the lyrics tell - looking out of my window, watching the seagulls and wishing I could be that free. This is a real 'standing on the platform with your suitcases' song.

Instrument: guitar. Tuning: EADGBE

```
Dm
As I look out of my window,
            C      G          Dm
I see the birds    in the sky,

How I wish that I could be them,
              C   G       Dm
So I could fly      far away.
```

**Chorus**

```
D                            FsharpM
Far away would I fly,
                          Bm
And I'd never look back to where I've been,
  Gm                                   D
I never plan on being there again.
                                       FsharpM
And the world keeps turning,

                             Bm
So I think I'll just fly on and when I land,
    Gm                               D
I'll dust myself off and start again.
```

So much has gone behind me,
And so much more lies ahead,
If I could look into the future?
Don't think I would, is what I said.

So look out of your window,
Can you see the birds in the sky?
Do you wish that you could be them,
So you could fly far away?

My first pub gig. 11 years old. Isle of Wight 1976.

# The Selkie

## (Damh the Bard)

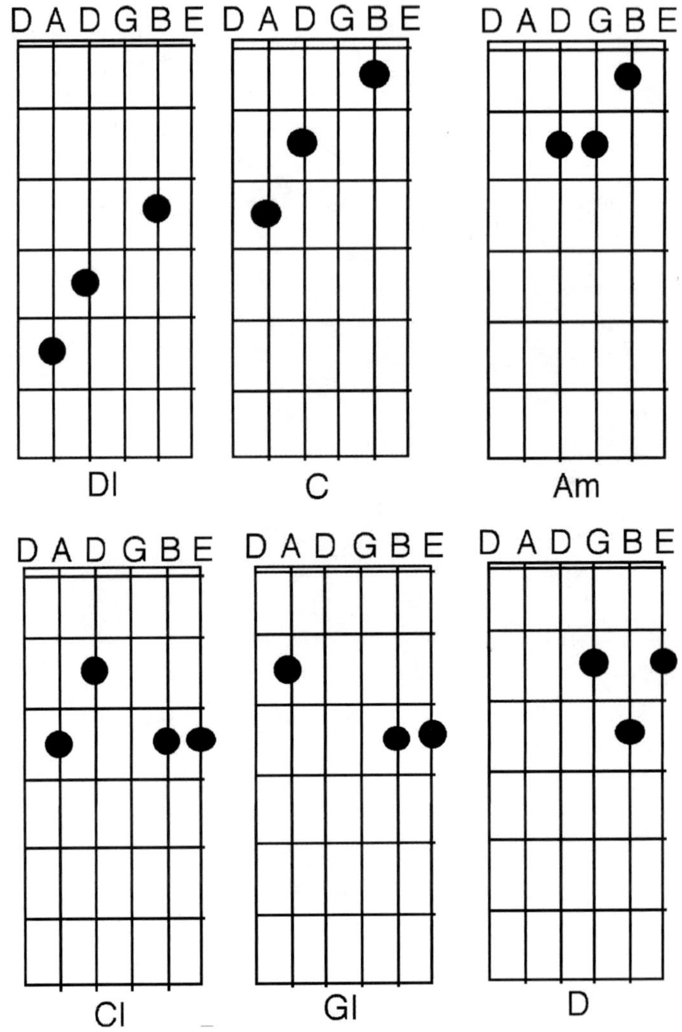

The story of a man who feels trapped by his life, and yearns to see freedom and love walking towards him through the waves.

Instrument: guitar. Tuning: DADGBE (Finger picked)

DI
Watch the ocean rolling in,
                                        C
Moonlight tripping off the waves,
            DI
Along the bays.

Like a mirror between the worlds,
                                      C
I catch the reflection of a star,
                                   DI
But it slips through my fingers.
Am
Then out from the water,

From out of the waves,
      C
Two eyes are looking at me.

**(Chorus 1)**
D    CI                                      GI
Oh,     I want to go to the sea again,
D    CI                                              GI          D      CI
Oh,       where the Selkies dance and I don't feel alone.
                                           DI
I want to go to the sea again.

Water dripping from flowing hair,
White horses gallop upon the shore,
Then canter once more,
Leave your skin upon the beach,
Free your mind and dance with me.
Within the sea.
I turn back to look at the places I know,
But my Selkie Woman calls to me,
And I go.

So I run into the waves,
where my Selkie is waiting for me,
And together we swim.
She takes me into her world,
Where I am her King and she is my Queen,
I have always lived here.
What could awake me from out of this sleep,
Could that be the dawning Sun?
No, No!

**(Chorus 2)**
Oh, I want to go to the sea again,
Oh, where the Selkies dance and I don't feel alone.
Tonight I'll go down to the sea again.

Me 18 years old with my Nan

# Winds of Change
## (Damh the Bard)

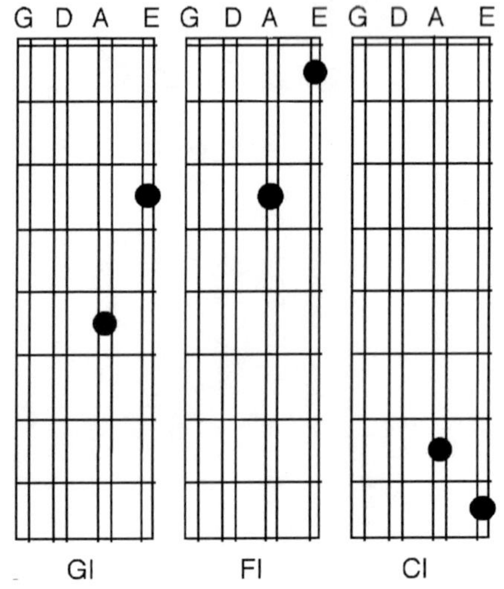


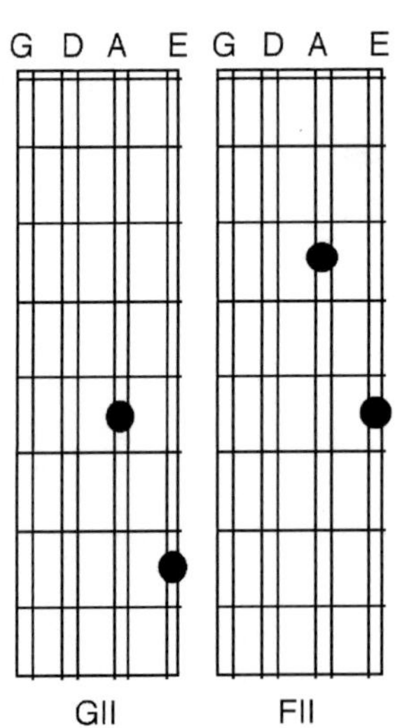

This is a song of hope.

Instrument: bouzouki. Tuning: GDAE

GI                                                                    FI
Feel the Winds of Change blow around your head,
                                          CI                          GII
And slowly they disappear, leaving a single thread,
                                                                  FI
You walk along this road to see where it leads,
                                             CI
To trouble or a brand-new day,
                                     GII
The future is there to take.

**(Chorus)**
GII                FII
Spread your wings,
CI              GII              FII
Live your life, can you hear me?
             GII     FII          CI           GII                 FII
Set you Spirit free, and live your life, can you hear me,
                     GI
Calling your name?

And though the Mists of Time, they cloud your view,
With one breath of life,
You can see where the path leads you.
You walk along this road to see what you find,
Those burdens on your back aren't yours,
You can leave them all behind.

The voice inside of your head is the Spirit of the Land,
So come and walk the Ancient Ways,
Reach out and take my hand.
You've walked this Path before
But you've never felt it so strong,
So let your heart be free,
Right here is where you belong!

Me playing with The Next Band -
Haywards Heath 6th Form College, 1982

# Lady of the Silver Wheel
## (Damh the Bard)

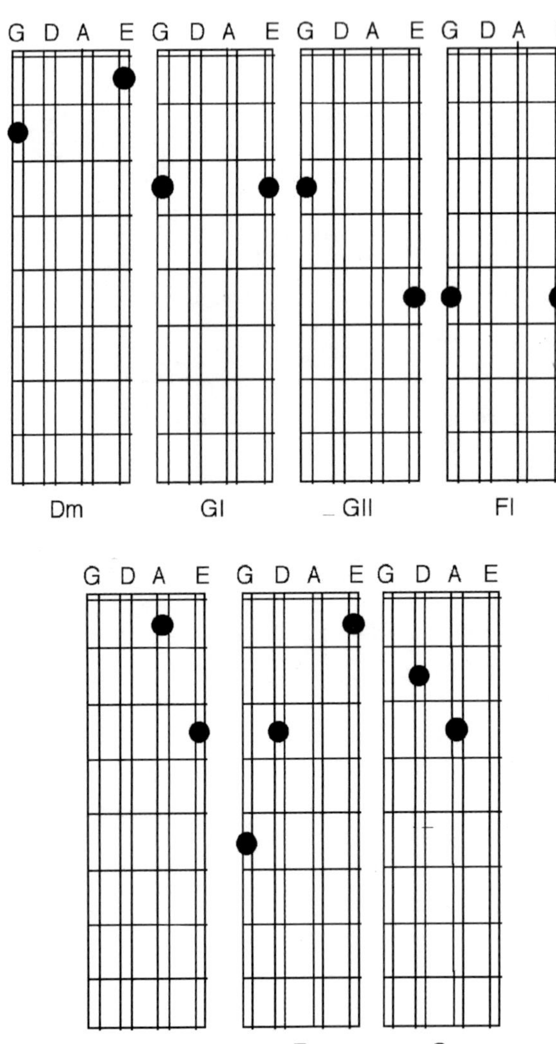

I had written three songs about Blodeuwedd, and wanted to write a song dedicated to her darker sister, Arianrhod. She was my guide through my Ovate grade studies with the OBOD, so this is my gift to you, Lady of Changes.

Instrument: mandolin. Tuning: GDAE

```
Dm          GI                GII
High in the Castle of Glass,
                FI            Dm
A Silver Wheel turns in the night,
                GI                GII
Slender hands guide a thread,
            FI               Dm
Keeping it true, keeping it tight,
            GI            GII
As it spins, fate it begins,
             FI
To opens its eyes,
      Dm           GI           GII
Lady of the Moon, of the Stars,
             FI                   Gm
In the Spiral Castle I hear you sing.
```

**(Chorus)**

```
Gm          Dm              Gm
Lady of the Silver Wheel,
            Dm          Gm
Lady of the Silver Wheel,
          Dm                      F                C                Dm
Arianrhod, Lady of Changes you spin the Web of Life, the Web of Life.
```

Gather up every thread,
Weave them together, join them as one,
The spindle begins to turn,
A soul's new journey has begun
On the Earth, with every birth,
So the web that joins together all life
Is as one, daughter and son,
Animal, human, old and young.

Autumn begins to fall,
And the Moon wanes and seasons grow cold.
We all hear the Raven's call,
Some while young, others grow old,
Oh she sings, the last chorus begins,
With a voice as gentle as Winter's Lace,
A new thread through the wheel it is fed,
Woe to those who see her face.

Me playing drums with Stride - Kings Head, Cuckfield, 1983

# Samhain Eve
## (Damh the Bard)

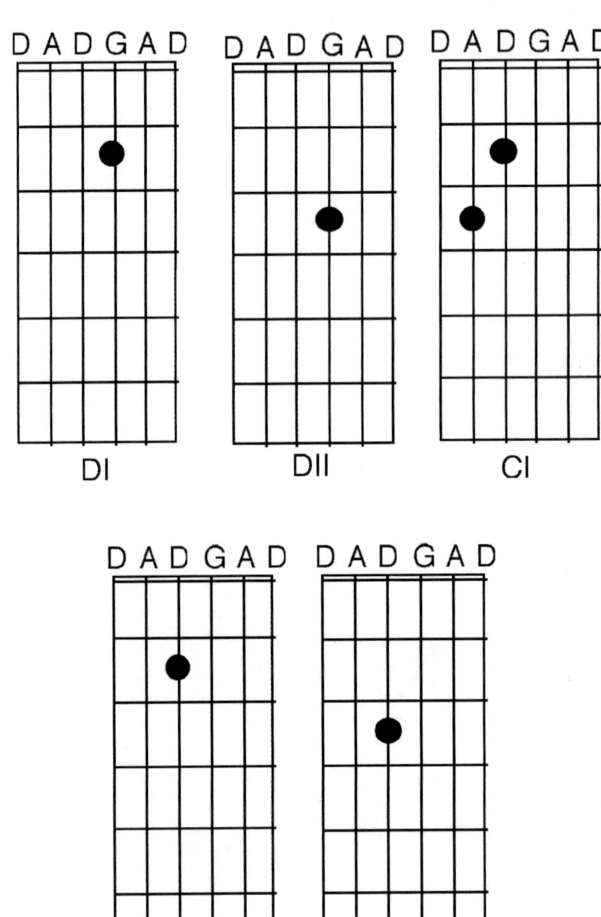

Modern Halloween can seem a little commercial these days, but there was a time when, for some, this night was filled with fear. Some of the old Celtic tales tell of the way that, at Samhain, the veil between the world is at its thinnest. The Faerie, and the dead walk this earth once more. So let's bring a bit more of the fear-factor into this sacred night, but not a fear borne of fright, but of awe.

Instrument: guitar. Tuning: DADGAD

```
DI         DII          DI      DII
Close the door, keep out the storm,
CI      AI  CI   AI      DI
Far away, far away,
           DII         DI           DII
Keep the need-fires burning til dawn,
GI   AI   CI         DI    DII   DI   DII   DI
Oh,       leave my soul.
         DII        DI          DII
For the cold will come this night,
     CI    AI  CI   AI   DI
From far away, far away,
           DII       DI        DII     GI   AI  CI         DI
Frost will fall ,and ice will bite,     Oh       leave my soul.
```

**Bridge 1:**

DII  AI  DII        AI
Oh        leave my soul,
DII                  AI            DI
Please pass me by when the evening falls,
DII  AI  DII          AI
Oh        blessed are we,
    DII        AI
The Taker of Souls we shall see.
               DI
On Samhain Eve.

I can hear the Hunter's hounds
Far away, far away,
I will cast the Circle round,
Oh leave my soul.
Raven-witch I feel your breath,
Far away, far away,
Bringing with you Summer's death,
Oh leave my soul.

Sunrise, the tolling bell,
Far away, far away,
Breaks the Raven-witches spell,
Oh blessed are we.
The leaves of the Oaken King,
Fade away, fade away,
Feed the seeds that will come in Spring
Oh blessed are we.

**Bridge 2:**
Oh blessed are we,
Summer will come with the May on the tree,
Oh hail to the Queen,,
And under the Sun we shall sing,
To call in the Spring.

(Cailleach)
Can you hear me calling you?
Can you hear me calling you?
Can you hear me calling and crying your name in the dark?
Can you hear me calling you?
Can you hear me calling you?
Can you hear me calling and crying your name in the dark?
I am the Shadow who calls to your soul.

# Ever With Me

## (Damh the Bard)

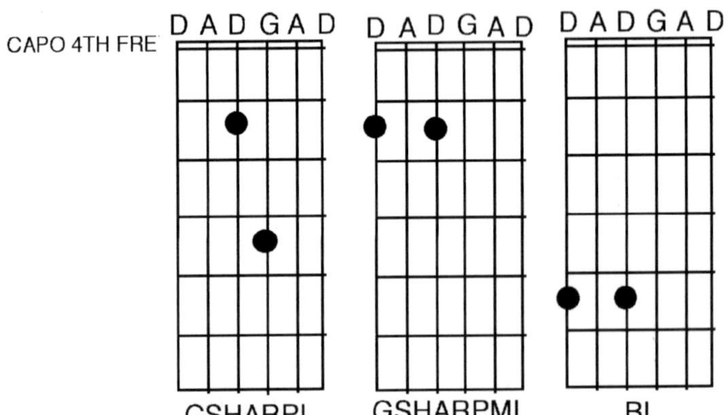


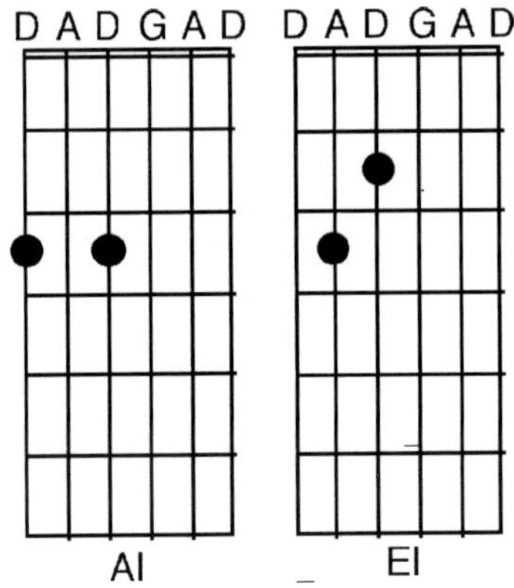

I wrote this song for Cerri, who was with me when I went through a very difficult stage in my life. As I wrote the words, and sang the final song through, I realised once more the importance of faith - faith in love and in friendship, to see us though those difficult times..

Instrument: guitar. Tuning: DADGAD. Capo: 4th fret

```
CsharpI                GsharpMI    BI
Sailing miles on an endless sea,
                             CsharpI
The shoulders of the ocean carry me.
                   GsharpMI        BI
A sign of land, a haven shore,
                                    CsharpI                GsharpMI
My sails catch the wind and I'm home once more.
        BI                  CsharpI                EI
A tired sailor coming home from war.
                         BI
I can ride the storm        because I know that...
```

**Chorus**

```
CsharpI                                   AI
She is ever with me, ever with me,
                   BI
The way that the Sun shines,
       Csharp I                          AI
She is ever with me, ever with me,
                   BI                    CsharpI
The way that the Sun shines, ever with me.
```

She was there through the darkest times,
When the sunlight didn't seem to shine,
Took my hand and she led me through,
The maze I had fallen in to,
And in the centre I stand with you.
I feel alive again, because I know that....

Now I watch the sands of time,
Slip through my fingers as it passes by,
In this life I can call my own,
For I know that I am not alone,
She will find me and lead me home.
And through the passing years I know that...

Me playing drums with Stride. King Edward Hall, Lindfield, 1984

# Grímspound

## (Damh the Bard)

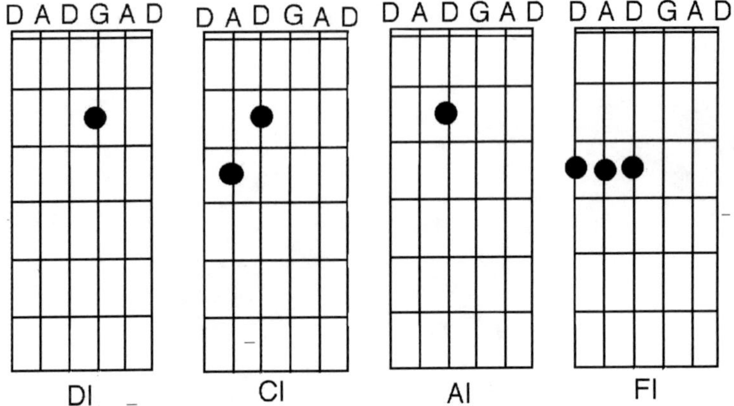

Grimspound is a late bronze age/early iron age settlement on Dartmoor. The roundhouses can be seen within the compound. I was having a real problem with writer's block - I had loads of tunes, but no lyrics. So one day I took myself and my guitar off to Dartmoor, sat in the largest roundhouse, communed with the Spirit of Place, and this song was the result. I would thoroughly recommend visiting the site, it is breathtakingly awesome.

Instrument: guitar. Tuning: DADGAD

DI            CI
Deep in the wildland,
DI            AI
Placed by a cold hand,
   DI            CI
A tribe of the heartland,
               AI
A world far away.
      DI          CI
The forest surrounds them,
       DI              AI
And Spirits have found them,
        DI                 CI
They drink from the fountain,
                        DI
On the noon of the day.

**(Chorus)**

```
      FI              CI
The wind and the rain,
             FI             CI
They still whisper its name,
           FI                    CI
And the name that they whisper,
     DI
Grimspound
```

I hear voices singing,
And fires they are burning,
The young they are learning,
From the Elders of the Tribe,
The brands they are lifted,
The names they are gifted,
And the initiated,
Are welcomed inside.

The trees they have fallen,
Ravens' lamentation,
The ghosts they still wander,
Within these fallen walls,
I feel your eyes on me,
Your spirit will still be,
Here for all to see,
Through the circles of time.

Me playing guitar with Stride. King Edward Hall, Lindfield, 1984

# The Ballad of John Barleycorn
## (Traditional arr. Damh the Bard)

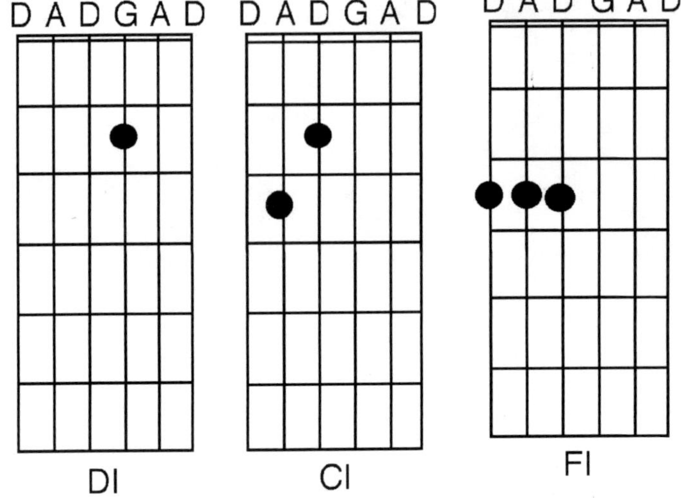

Instrument: guitar. Tuning: DADGAD

DI                                        FI
There were three men came out of the West
        CI                    DI
Their fortunes for to try
                                              FI
And these three men made a solemn vow
        CI                      DI
John Barleycorn must die.
       FI                                    CI
They ploughed, they sowed, they harrowed him in
         FI                        CI
Threw clods all upon his head
      DI                                    FI
And these three men made a solemn vow
        CI                      DI
John Barleycorn was Dead.

They let him stand for a very long time
Till the rains from heaven did fall
Then little Sir John's sprung up his head
And so amazed them all
They let him stand till the Midsummer Day
Till he grew both pale and wan
Then little Sir John's grew a great, long beard
And so become a man.

They hire'd men with scythes so sharp
To cut him off at the knee.
They bound him and tied him around the waist
Serving him most barb'rously.
They hire'd men with their sharp pitch-forks
To prick him to the heart
But the drover served him worse than that
For he's bound him to a cart.

They rolled him around and around the field
Till they came unto a barn
And these three men made a solemn mow
Of poor John Barleycorn
They hire'd men with crab-tree sticks
To strip him skin from bone
But the miller, served him worse than that,
For he's ground him between two stones.

Here's Little Sir John in the nut-brown bowl
And brandy in the glass
But Little Sir John in the nut-brown bowl's
Proved the stronger man at last
For the hunts man he can't hunt the fox
Nor cheerily blow his horn
And the tinker, can't mend Kettle or pot
Without a little Barleycorn.

# The Hills they are Hollow
## (Damh the Bard)

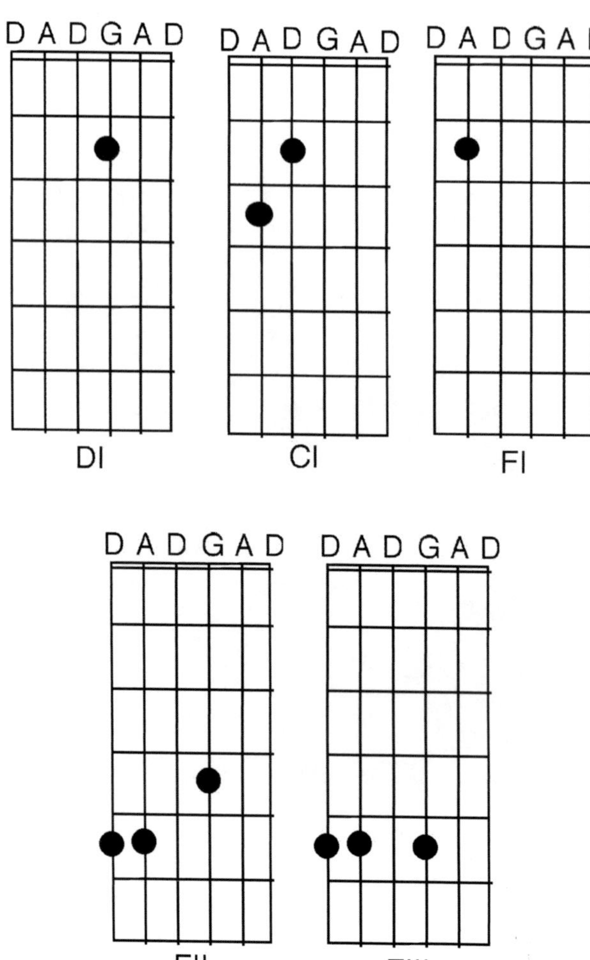

I wrote this on the same day as Grimspound, during my visit to Dartmoor. This song was written whilst sitting in the stone circle at Merrivale on Dartmoor and, like the Song of Awen, really sums up my view of Spirit.

Instrument: guitar. Tuning: DADGAD

```
DI
As I walk upon this green land,

This land that love,
        CI
I see figures of chalk,
           FI                    DI
Carved into the hillsides above.

Cerne Abbas a man so proud,
                                           CI
And the Long Man opens wide the gates of his world,
       FI                      DI
And invites you to step inside.
```

**(Chorus)**

```
FII                                FIII        FII
And the hills they are hollow and home to the Fey,
       DI
Who dance on Midsummer's Eve,
       FII                 FIII           FII
Some people don't understand when I say,
DI
These are the things I believe.
```

These are the things I believe.
There is an old circle of stones,
That stands on the moor,
Every moss-covered face,
Tells the secrets of ancient lore.
The Tors stand as guardians,
Witnesses to the Rites of Nature's Gods,
Of Darkness and of Light.

Let's sing of the mystery,
Of Sacred Land,
See the shapes in the corn,
Made by invisible hands,
Secrets of the Pagan Ways,
Lie all around,
Written upon the Earth,
In rock and Sacred Mound!

Me in Eclipse. Haywards Heath 6th Form College, 1984.

# Land of the Ever Young

## (Damh the Bard)

Capo 2nd fret

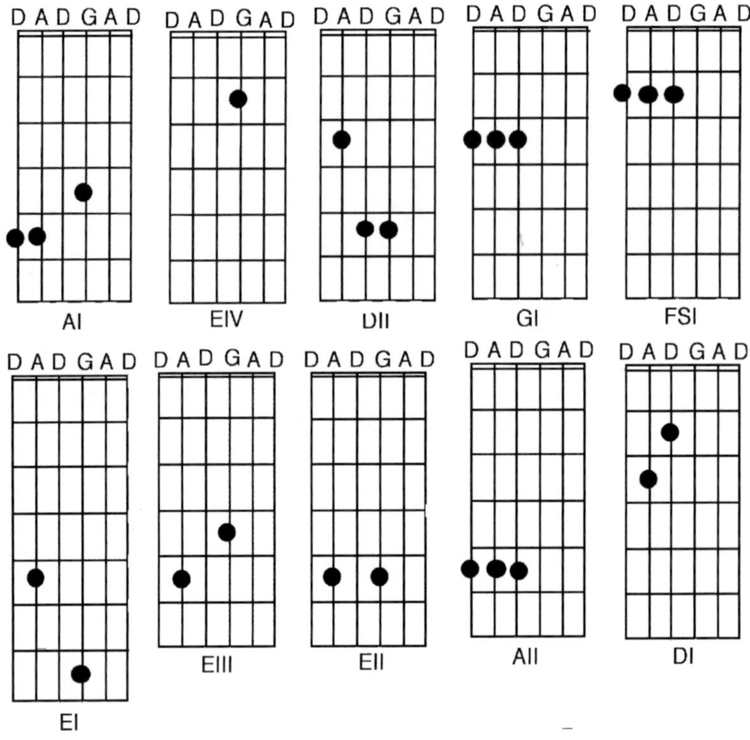

This song is an autobiography of my spiritual life, and contains my interaction with the Stag, the Fey, the sea, and Seagull. Come sing with me....

Instrument: guitar. Tuning: DADGAD. Capo 2nd fret

EI                          EII
I thought that I'd never see,
                               EIII
All the wonder and mystery,
     EII
All around me, around me,
       EI                    EII
Then I met the Spirit of the Stag,
                         EIII
And I climbed upon his back,
             EII
When he found me, he found me.

**(Bridge)**
             DII  AI          EIV
And Now, I             can never return,
        DI    AI            EIV
To the way   I once had been,
     DI    AI                     EIV
For I            have been to the Land of the Young,

          DII              AI
Take my hand, Follow me,
          EIV
Hear our song....

**(Chorus)**

GI
Come with me and I'll take you away,
DI EIV
To the Land of the Ever Young,
GI
Through the hills to the home of the Fey,
DI FSI
Where the air is warmed by the Sun,
AII
It's all around just listen,
EIV DI AI
And I will take you there.
EIV DI AI
Take you there.

I felt the power of the sea,
Of Manannan's great City,
All around me, around me,
Then I swam deep among Apple trees,
The tide like the gentle breeze,
All around me, around me.

I raise my feathered wings,
Hear the wind and the song she sings,
All around me, around me,
And I know the freedom of the skies,
Up here where the Seagull flies,
All around me, around me.

# Only Son
## (Damh the Bard)

Capo 2nd fret

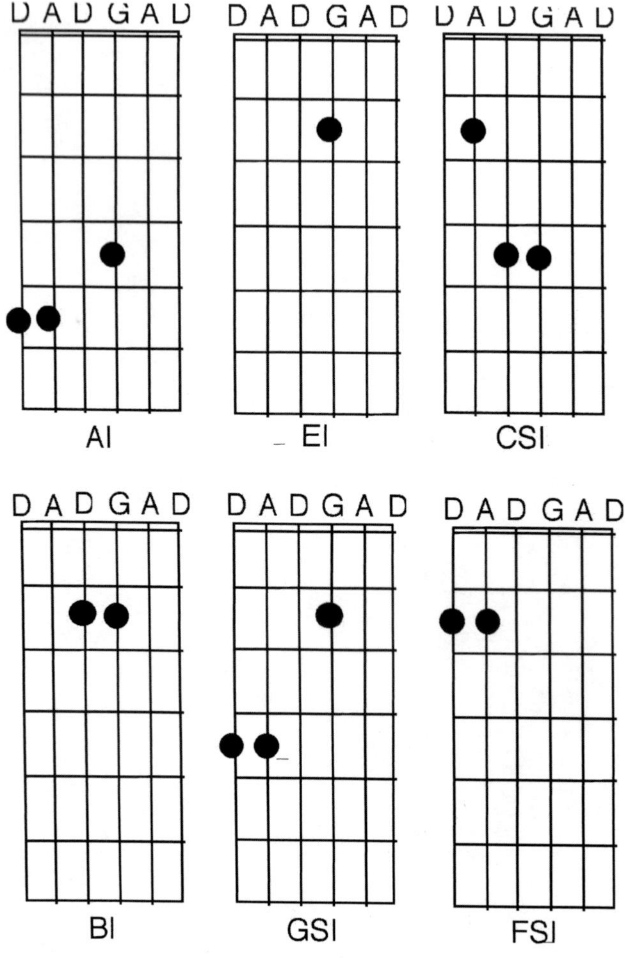

This song was originally going to be called Herne's Apprentice, about an apprentice, and his Shaman teacher walking into a forest as the old Shaman prepares to move on. But as I wrote the song, it developed into a touching dialogue between Father and Son. A tear jerker, this one...

Instrument: guitar. Tuning: DADGAD. Capo 2nd fret

EI GSI FSI
Take your time,
AI EI GSI FSI AI EI
Cause I can't walk any faster,
GSI FSI
With every step you take you'll find,
AI EI GSI FSI AI BI
That my time is drawing closer.
AI BI
And all I've said and all I've done,
AI EI GSI
You are my friend, my only Son.

**(Chorus)**
FSI
And I love you,
AI EI GSI
You're my friend, my only Son,
FSI
I'm your Father,
AI
Please don't look away,
CSI AI
For the dark of the night will give way to a bright new day.

Take my hand,
For this journey is almost over,
I can see the Western Lands,
And their hills are clad in clover.
I swear by blood, I swear by bone,
That you will never be alone.

Beside this stream,
With its gentle waters flowing,
I close my eyes to end this dream,
With Spring's new leaves unfurling,
And when the Lady calls your name,
I'll hold you in my arms again.

Me in my more hippy outfit. Eclipse, Haywards Heath 6th Form College, 1985

# The Mabon
## (Damh the Bard)

Capo 2nd fret

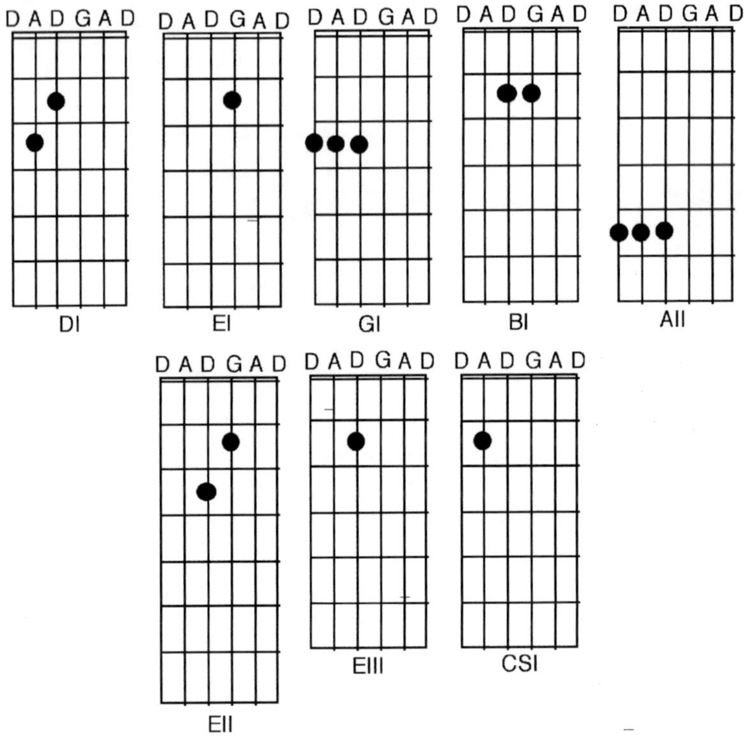

With this song I wanted to capture the animalistic, and wild aspects of the Pagan paths. I was picturing the night of the Winter Solstice, when all over the planet Pagans gather to celebrate the rebirth of the Sun Child, the Mabon. I also wanted to give a feel that he, too, was watching us......

Instrument: guitar. Tuning: DADGAD. Capo 2nd fret

```
EI
Twisting shapes in the moonlight
             GI             DI              EI
I hear the rhythm of the distant Pagan drums,
               GI      DI
Within the hills,
EI
Shadows dance in the sunlight,
             GI           DI                 EI
I feel the power of the wise and ancient ones,
               GI      DI
Now I must go.
(Climb)
AII
Beyond the world we see,
          GI              DI
Where Spirit runs with bull and stallion,
AII
Cross Earth and Sky and Sea,
      GI           BI
The Mabon I shall be.
```

**(Chorus)**

EII EIII DI CSI EII
By Earth and Water, Air and Fire,
EIII DI CSI EII
With blood and spirit and desire,
EIII DI CSI EII EIII DI
A fire in my head I will wear the antlered crown.

Fires burning at midnight,
Across the world I hear my story being told,
Father and Son.
Chanting voices at midnight,
Are singing songs about the power that I hold,
The newborn Sun.

**(Chorus)**

By Earth and Water, Air and Fire,
With blood and spirit and desire,
A fire in my head I will wear the antlered crown.
And in the forest dance with me,
And in your heart you shall be free,
For I am you, and you shall find,
That you are me.

Shadows cast in the sunlight,
I see my children turn their eyes towards the sky,
Towards the Sun.
Dawn of life in the sunlight,
Mithras, Osiris, Dionysis, Herne and Pan,
We all are one.

# Merlín am I
## (Damh the Bard)

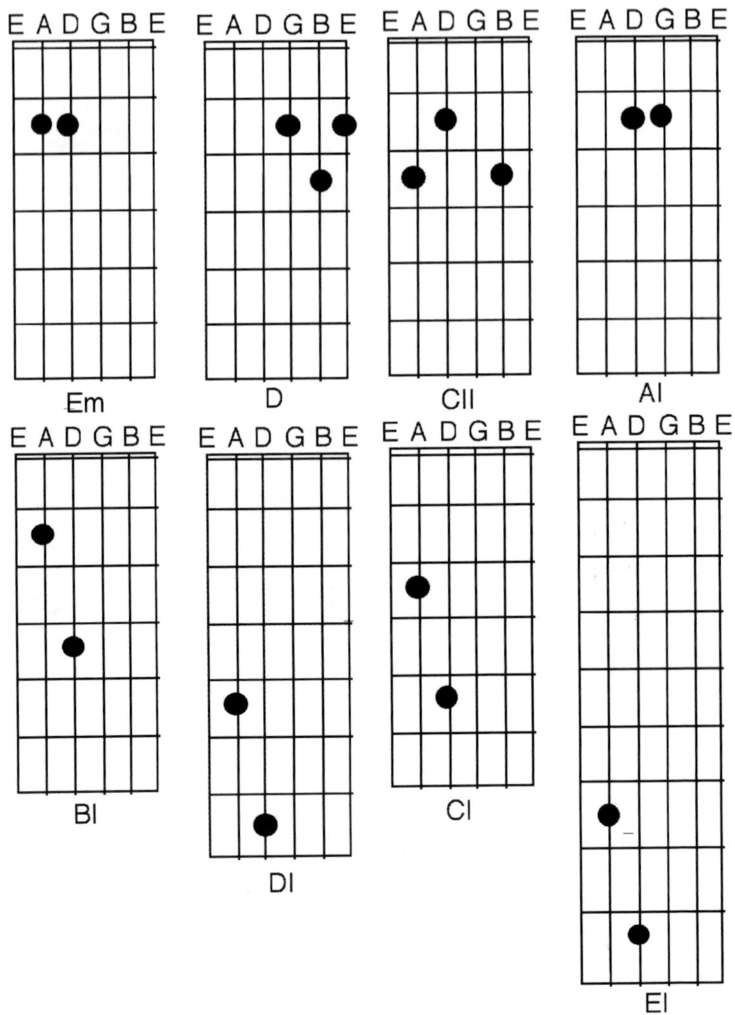

Merlin has always been a fascination of mine ever since I was a child. He was with me through my Druid grade studies with the OBOD, and I really wanted to tell his story through song. This is not the Arthurian Merlin, but the Shaman Druid, whose tale lives on in the very rock of Clas Myrdhin, the Island of the Mighty, Merlin's Isle.

Instrument: guitar. Tuning: EADGBE

EI                    DI                 EI
In a tower on the western shore,
                      BI      CI
A woman cries in pain,
                    DI
Outside a storm gathers,
      EI              BI      EI
As a soul is born again.
                  DI
The wisdom of all the worlds,
EI                              BI      CI
Shines like the Sun from his eyes,
                DI
His Father a God of the Earth,
          EI                          BI
Holds his Mother in his arms as she dies.

**(Chorus)**

Em                D                  CII<br>
Merlin am I, Merlin am I,<br>
                  D<br>
I know the secrets,<br>
            Em<br>
Of the land and the sky,<br>
D<br>
Land and the sky,<br>
                  CII<br>
And you'll hear my voice,<br>
            D<br>
In the eagle's cry,<br>
                  EI<br>
Merlin am I.

A tower to the High King,<br>
Comes crashing to the ground,<br>
His Druids know the answer,<br>
A sacrifice is found.<br>
But the child sees deep in the Earth,<br>
Two Dragons are spreading their wings,<br>
Two tribes will fight for to claim this land,<br>
Many die for the folly of Kings.

Listen little pig,<br>
Little trembling one,<br>
Under this blanket I find no repose.<br>
Since the battle of Arderydd,<br>
I no longer care,<br>
If the sky falls,<br>
Or the sea overflows.

The forest is calling him,
From a field soaked in blood,
Where hundreds lie dying,
All the people he loved,
Now he runs in the shadows,
And madness, the future reveals,
That the Island of Britain is Merlin's Isle,
And he lives here still.

# The Greenwood Grove

## (Damh the Bard)

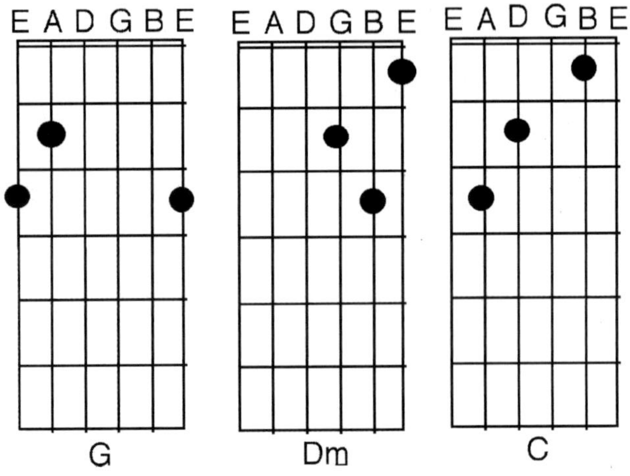


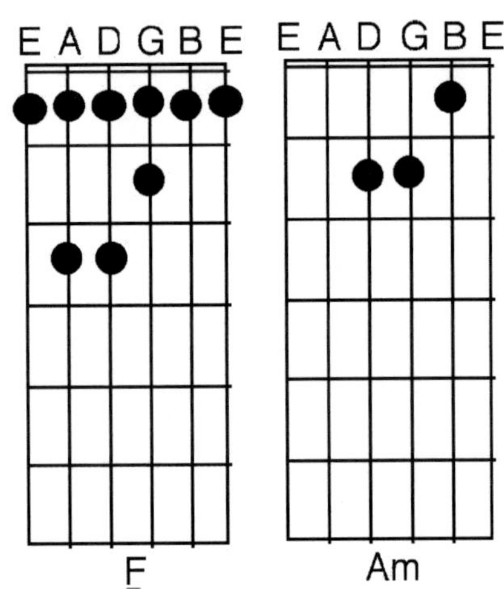

I had the tune, and title, of this song for ages, but simply couldn't find the words! Then I thought about the Celtic Ogham, and words began to be whispered into my ear, as the pen began to flow. It is the complete 20 tree Ogham, in order, sung as a Bardic nmemonic.

Instrument: GUITAR. Tuning: EADGBE

```
Dm                     C              Dm    C    Dm
I am the Birch of the new beginnings,
                       C              Dm    C    Dm
The Rowan star with magic guarding,
F                C                Dm     C    Dm
Alder sight the future showing,
                         C              Dm     C     Am
Sweet Willow sees her Moon arising,
Dm                     C            Dm      C     Dm
Ash the three realms he is touching,
                        C              Dm     C     Dm
Hawthorn tells us the May is coming,
F                  C                     Dm      C    Dm
Mighty Oak with strength is standing,
                   C              Dm        C     Am
The Holly on his chariot riding.
```

**(Chorus)**

```
F              C   Dm             C
Come follow me, come dance with me,
Dm                 C                          Am         Dm
Come with me to the Greenwood Grove such magic there to see.

F                 C      Dm            C
The Lord of the Wild, with his Faerie kin,
Dm             C
Deep within the Greenwood Grove,
      Am            Dm
We'll dance the Magic Ring.
```

Wise Hazel watches the salmon feeding,
The Faerie Apple seed is falling,
The Vine is ripe intoxicating,
I am the Ivy heed my warning,
Yellow Broom I offer healing,
Blackthorn sharp for death preparing,
The Elder is a life of learning,
Fir the distant future showing.

I am the gorse I am destroying,
Heather from death recreating,
Hear the Aspen's leaves a-whispering,
That Yew is death and life returning.

# Spirit of Albion
## (Damh the Bard)

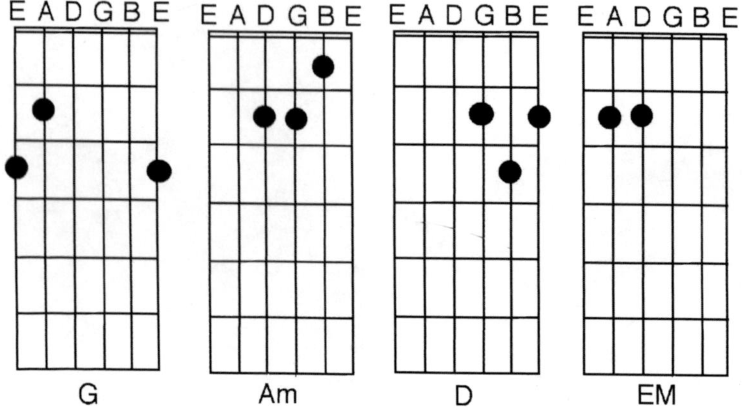

I wrote this song after an encounter with a Welsh nationalist. I love this island - from the Glens of the Highlands, to the moors of the West Country, to the fens of East Anglia, to the mountains of Snowdonia - I see them all as parts of my home. I don't profess to own any of it, if anything, the land owns me.

Instrument: guitar. Tuning: EADGBE

```
Em
An isle so fair, an isle so green,
G              D       Em
Known by many names.

Feel the pulse, the pulse of the land,
               G            D          Em        G
The blood boils within your veins.
Am
Someone go down to the Holy Well
       Em
and raise the Spirits there!
Am
Lay a feather on a stone,
           D
with a flame, and a lock of hair.
```

**(Chorus)**

```
Em
The crane, the wolf, the bear and the boar,
             G
No longer dwell upon these shores,
      Am
You say the Goddess and God have gone,
       D
Well I tell you they live on!
                           Em
For in the cities and hills,
                      G
And in circles of stone,
      Am
The voices of the Old Ways,
      D                                 Em
The Spirit of Albion is calling you home!
```

From Manwydden's crashing sea,
To the moor and the Highland Glen.
From the Faerie Hills, home of the Sidhe,
To the veins of the Broad and the Fen.
Someone go down to the Holy Trees
of Oak and Ash and Thorn!
Utter a charm in the verse of three,
Till the Summer King is born!

Ride the white horses
carved into the hills,
Walk to the Hanging Stones.
Bow to the might
of Cerne Abbas' height,
Feel the peace in the Ancestors' homes.
Someone go down to Wilmington
where the Giant guards the way!
Step into the Otherworld,
into the womb,
Where centuries pass like a day!

# Taliesin's Song

(Damh the Bard)

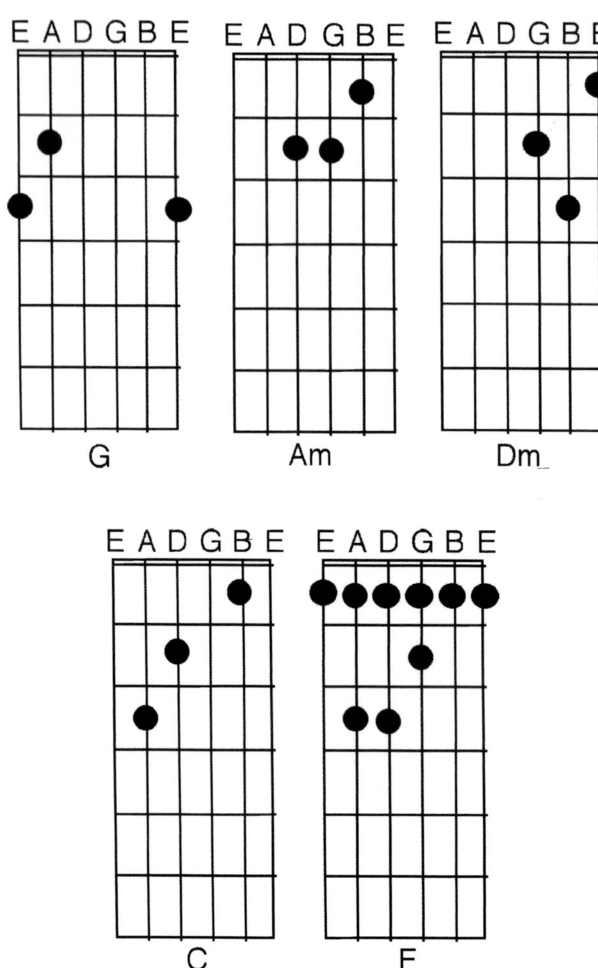

Taliesin was/is such an inspiration of mine, especially when I first began to explore the Path of the Bard. I imagined sitting in the old King's moot hall, as the Great Bard stepped in, shook his Silver Branch, and began to tell his stories.

Instrument: guitar. Tuning: EADGBE

```
Dm           F
I was in the court of kings,
  C                   Am
I saw great halls and countless gems,
      Dm                  C     Am
T'was where I heard Taliesin sing,
       Dm
Of the love of women
        C         Dm
and the deeds of men.
                  F
The Awen's light filled his eyes,
  C                Am
A fire burned within his head,
      Dm                   C         Am
As he sang of times long past and cried,
    Dm                  C    Dm
For Merlin, Arthur and Galahad.
```

**(Chorus)**

```
F              C
Manwydden, Cerridwen,
          G             Dm
The Old Ones let us sing to them,
F                       Dm
Arianrhod, Bran and Bel.
F              C
Blodeuwedd, Cealleach,
     G                       Dm
The Old Gods they are coming back.
F                                  Dm
Listen people to the tales I tell.
```

I have been a crashing wave,
A stallion across the sea,
And I have been a rutting stag,
And I hold Albion's destiny.
The Cauldron deep in Annwn's mist,
With Blackthorn staff
I travelled there,
And Arthur whom fate did kiss,
The Seven Castles we did dare!

I have seen the plants and trees,
Great Oak the Ash and sacred Thorn,
Bring Annwn's Host to its knees,
And suffer mighty Gwydion's scorn.
But still the fight could not be won,
Until they guessed the giant's name,
Ravens and Alder on his shield,
"By the branch you bear, Bran is your name!"

# On the Noon of the Solstice

## (Damh the Bard)

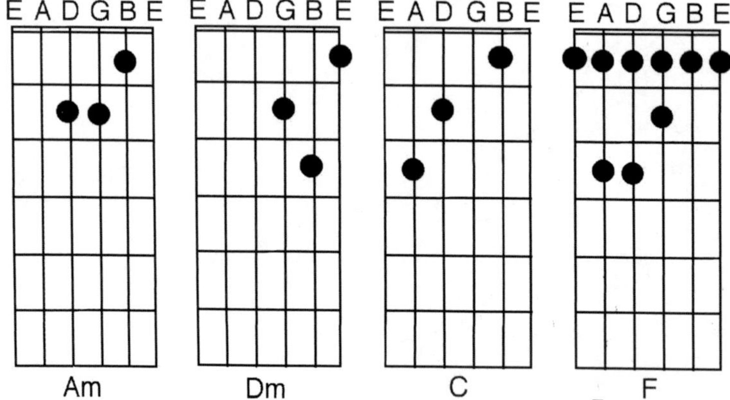

This was the second Pagan song I ever wrote. It was the time of the Summer Solstice, and I was walking my dog through local woods at Ditchling Common. The day was bright, and I began to hum a tune, then the chorus just appeared from out of the blue, quickly followed by the verses. Dedicated to Old Horny himself.

Instrument: guitar. Tuning: EADGBE

```
Dm                         C      Dm
In times long past lived a Man of green,
        F                          C
And his footsteps brought life wherever he'd been.
       Dm          C           Dm
In the deepest wildwood was the place he was seen,
                  C           Am
And the people did love and protect him.
         Dm           C                     Dm     Am
And they saw his face change, with the turn of the Wheel
       Dm           C              Dm
of the Seasons, They heard his voice sing.
```

**(Chorus)**

F
I'm the Horned God,
            C
I'm the face in the trees,
            Dm                  C                 Dm              Am
I'm the breath of the wind that rustles the leaves,
            F
I'm the Green Man
          C
in the wildwood I roam,
      Dm                C                  Dm
Cernunnos, I'm Pan and I'm Herne.

I shall be as the Dark Holly King,
Darkness and cold
in my cloak I will bring,
And on Winter's nights
to me you will sing,
Till the air around me starts changing,
And on the noon of the solstice
I'll give up my crown,
To the Light
and the Mighty Oak King.

All Summer long
I shall rule just and fair,
Bring your crops to fruit
with the light that I share,
With fire and water,
from earth into air,
But the Wheel it keeps
steadily turning.
And on the noon of the Solstice
I'll give up my crown,
To the cold and the Dark Holly King.

T'is now modern times
and the Summer is here,
The Winter has gone
and the air it is clear,
On a fine day I walked
through a woods I live near,
When a battle I spied
through a clearing,
Two giants of leaves,
one light and one dark,
Even now the Wheel it is turning!

# The Wheel
## (Damh the Bard)

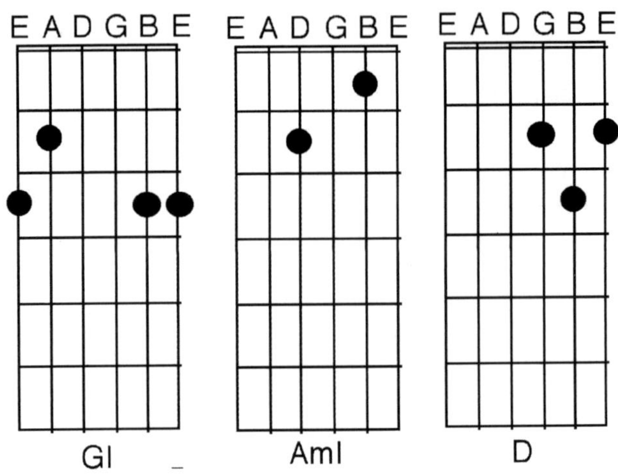


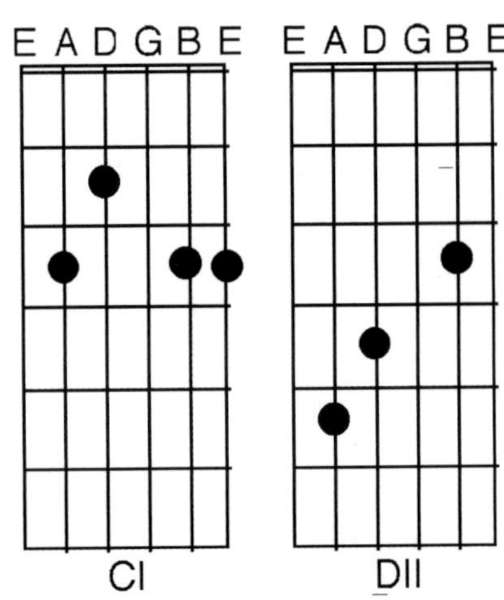

This song is a love song between the God and Goddess. It tells of the God's birth, their meeting, their love within the Greenwood, and his death, at her hands, in the corn fields. But he waits in the earth for her to return, and together they will rule in the Otherworld, until his rebirth in the Spring.

Instrument: guitar. Tuning: EADGBE (Finger Picked)

AmI
As the sunrise on the shortest day
                              DII          AmI
my crying greets the dawn.
                                                         DII        CI
Tears of dew form on the web As I am reborn.
                 GI                      D
Feel new life spring from the Earth,
         CI            GI                 D          CI
As the Mother of All Life gives birth.
                   GI              D                     AmI
Though I am a child I will soon become a man.
          DII            AmI
Aaaaaa-aaaaaah
          DII            AmI
Aaaaaa-aaaaaah

Feel the warmth upon your skin,
Sense the animal inside.
As every creature on the land,
Feels the rising tide.
The natural rhythms
of the land,
As the Goddess takes my hand,
Into the Forest Green
with the Horned Man.

The waves of corn
have turned to gold,
My time is drawing near.
I see my Lady smile at me,
Inside I feel no fear.
As She raises the scythe
above Her head.
Blood spills on the Earth
as I fall dead,
In the Otherworld
I guard Her throne
'til She returns

Me and my best friend Glen, 1983. I still have my Flying V guitar

# Oak, Broom & Meadowsweet

(Damh the Bard)

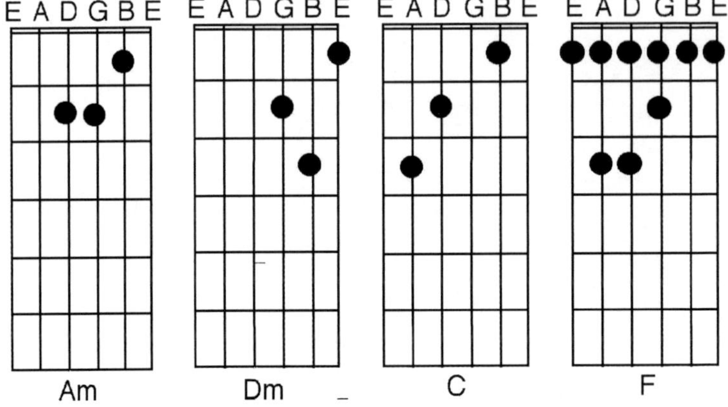

This is the first song in my Blodeuwedd trilogy, and was the first song I wrote around a Celtic myth. It has already had a wonderful life - being used as the basis for a large Beltane ceremony in the New Forest, and now sung by many in honour of the Spring Queen.

Instrument: guitar. Tuning: EADGAE

```
Dm               C               Dm          Am
Gather 'round people let me spin you a tale,
      Dm       C
Of a Mother's anger
                          Dm
and a curse doomed to fail.
                C            Dm         Am
Arianrhod's baby whom she did disown,
      Dm       C             Am          Dm
And Gwydion stole him to raise as his own.
                  C            Dm         Am
Well the boy he grew to be strong and brave,
         Dm     C
But his Mother cursed him
                     Dm
not to be given a name.

                  C               Dm          Am
When he cast a stone where a Wren it did land,
    Dm                 C                     Dm
She said, "The Young Lion has a Steady Hand!"
```

**(Chorus)**

```
            F                  C
Call the May, Call the May,
            Dm                 Am
Call the May, Call the May,
Dm                C                           Dm
Gather 'round people and call in the May.
            F                  C
Call the May, Call the May,
            Dm                 Am
Call the May, Call the May,
Dm                C                           Dm
Gather 'round people and call in the May.
```

So she laid upon him a new destiny,
"You shall never have any weapons
unless given by me".
Then a phantom army by Gwydion's charms,
Forced Arianrhod to give Llew his arms.
Then in rage and torment
she laid down this curse,
"You shall never marry a woman
of the race of the Earth".
So Gwydion and Math planned
to foil her hate,
And with the herbs of the forest
they twisted his fate.

So they gathered from the forest,
from the Grove where they meet,
Flowers of Oak, Broom and Meadowsweet.
And uttering upon them a Verse of Power,
A figure began to form from the flowers.
Oh rise, and wake, fairest Lady of Spring!
Come and be wed to the Forest King!
Flower-face is your name oh Blodeuwedd,
You carry life within your breath!

Come Oak, broom and meadowsweet,
Come Oak, broom and meadowsweet,
Come Oak, broom and meadowsweet,
Come hawthorn, come May!
Come Oak, broom and meadowsweet,
Come Oak, broom and meadowsweet,
Come Oak, broom and meadowsweet,
Come Blodeuwedd, come wake!

# The Winter King

## (Damh the Bard)

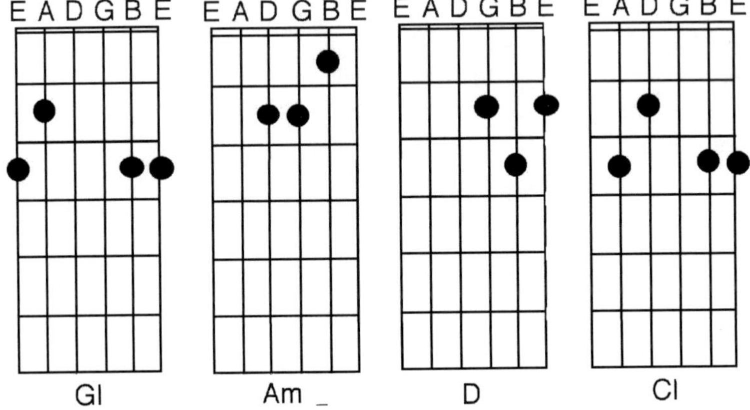

Just as it says, this song came to me whilst standing on the cliffs of Boscastle in Cornwall, overlooking the mighty Atlantic, feeling its power as the roar echoed around the cliffs. Within that sound you could almost hear a voice, telling the story of the Once and Future King.

Instrument: guitar. Tuning: EADGBE

D
Nah, nah, na-na, nah, nah

Nah, nah, na-na, nah, nah
CI                 GI          D
Nah, nah, na-na, na-na, nah

D
Facing the west to a distant land,
                              CI      GI
Gazing out to the sea,
D
Standing on Cornwall's rocky shore,
       CI                         D
The crashing waves far below me,

I heard a woman calling my name,

      CI                         D
Her voice the voice of a friend,
        Am                                    CI
And she said, "Now hear me, I'm Morgan le Fey,
         GI                              D
Let me tell you a story with no end."

The life of a man, the life of a King,
The love for a Queen,
Pendragon of Britain,
Sovereign of the Land,
The mightiest warrior ever seen.
The Magic Sword in his hand,
Like lightning, cut through the air.
A gift of the Goddess,
Lady of the Lake,
To Valiant Arthur, the Bear.

In the heart of Dumnonia
stands a tower,
An Isle on a sea of glass.
Where Merlin planned
the Old Gods of the Land,
Would return to Britain at last.
Twelve of the Thirteen Treasures were there,
Clyddno Eiddin's Cauldron
the quest,
On Prydwen they sailed,
Into the Otherworld,
None but seven
returned from the west.

Facing the west to a distant land,
Gazing out to the sea,
Standing on Cornwall's rocky shore,
The Crashing waves far below me,
I see a ship disappear in the mist,
That shines like silver and bronze,
Carrying the body
of the Wounded King,
To be healed in Avalon.

# Save Me
## (Damh the Bard)

Capo 2nd fret

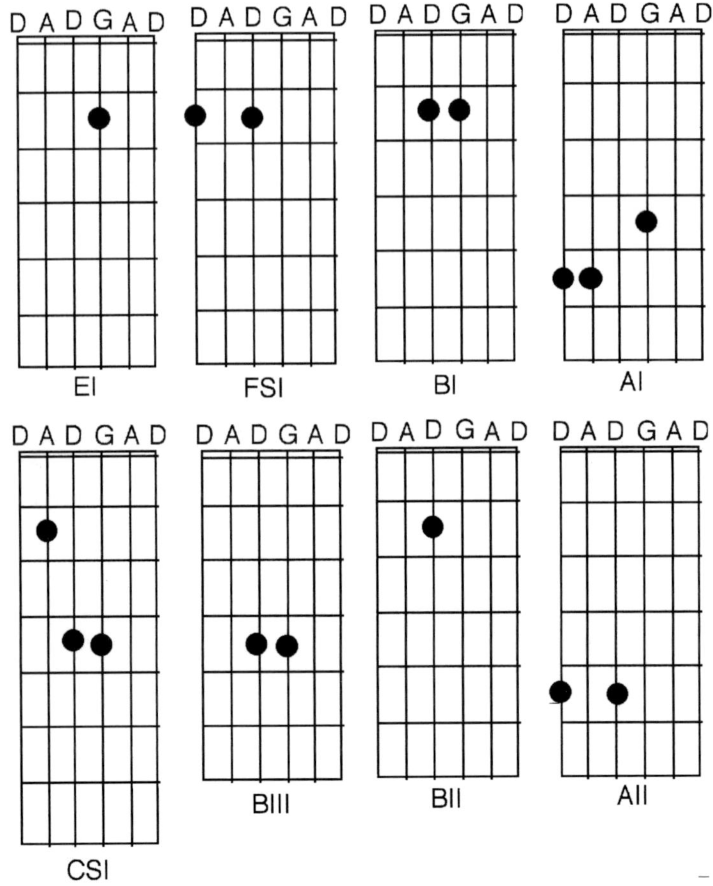

A song of hope, within despair.

Instrument: guitar. Tuning: DADGAD

```
EI                          BII
The young boy sat in his room,
          AI
Drawing circles on a page,
EI            BII
Spirals in the gloom,
             AI                          FSI
His Mother said, "Just act your age!"
                                AII
But his mind still dreams of Fairyland
                      EI     BII    AI  FSI
Of magic and mystery,
                             AII
Why does no one seem to understand,
                 BI
Or see what he sees.
```

**Chorus**

```
          CSI  BIII    AI
He says sa--------------ve me
CSI  BIII       AI
Sa--------------ve me
BII         AI  EI
Won't somebody save me?
```

Mirror on the wall,
Who is the fairest of them all?
The girl she was before,
A girl she can barely recall,
Or the old woman at her shoulder,
With sadness in her eyes,
Will she be her when she's older?
She hangs her head and cries.

And the light in your eyes says darling,
It'll be okay
Your life is there ready for you,
All you need to say, is…

An old photograph,
Of a girl he once knew,
She called yesterday,
What is he going to do?
He'll take the glass slipper,
Through hill and vale,
And happy ever after,
Will end the Fairy tale.

Me in 80s Glam Rock outfit with my lovely Ford Capri -
Cerri made me put this in!

# Domeana

## (Trad. Arr. Damh the Bard)

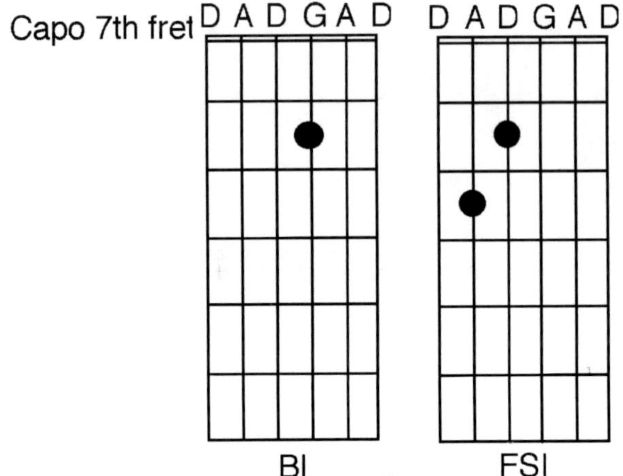

Another traditional 'Dirty sailor gets the posh bird' song.

Instrument: guitar. Tuning DADGAD        Capo 7th fret

```
BI                              FSI                BI
As Jack went a-walking      all on a fine day,
                                           FSI              BI
Well a Squire and his Lady came walking that way,
                        FSI      BI          FSI
And the Squire to the Lady did say,
    BI              FSI           BI          FSI
"Tonight with you love I mean to lay"
           BI
With me Domeana, demeana, domeana, day.
```

"Just tie a string, all around you finger,
And let the other end dangle down from your window.
And I'll come by and I'll pull the string,
And you'll come down and you'll let me in"
With me Domeana, demeana, domeana, day.

Jack says to himself, "I've a mind for to try,
And see if a poor sailor he can't win that prize."
So Jack walks by, and he pulls the string,
And she came down and she let old Jack in.
With his Domeana, demeana, domeana, day.

The Squire came a-riding, he was singing a song,
He was thinking to himself how it wouldn't be long,
But when he arrived no string he found,
And all of his hopes were all dashed to the ground.
With his Domeana, demeana, domeana, day.

It was early in the morning it was just getting light,
Well the Lady woke up with a terrible fright!
For there lay Jack in his tarry old shirt,
And behold his face was all covered in dirt,
With his Domeana, demeana, domeana, day.

"Oh what do you mean, you tarry sailor!
Sneaking in a Lady's chamber to steal her treasure!"
"Oh no," says Jack. "I just pulled a string,
And you came down and you let me in."
With me Domeana, demeana, domeana, day.

Jack says to the Lady, "Your pardon I pray,
I'll steal away very quietly at the break of the day."
"Oh no," she says, "Don't you go too far,
For I never will part from my Jolly Jack Tar,
And his Domeana, demeana, domeana, day."

Me with Glam/Thrash metal band, Targa. The Ship, Brighton,

# The Sun & the Rose
## (Damh the Bard)

Capo 2nd fret

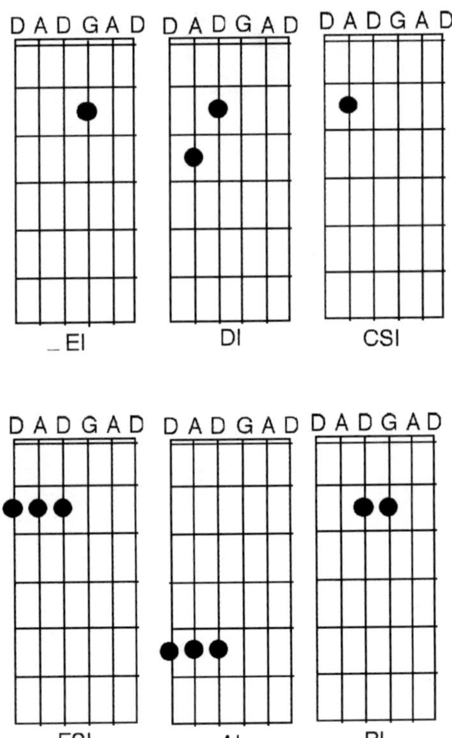

Instrument: guitar. Tuning DADGAD. Capo 2nd fret

FSI         AI               EI
Look at the Sun, see how he shines,
            DI    CSI         FSI
Lighting up every part of our lives,
           AI                EI
Calling the life, out from the dark,
             DI     CSI       FSI
Climbing up higher into the light,
           AI           EI
I wonder if he, feels like me,
  DI          CSI     FSI
A Sun in the sky all alone,
            AI          EI
Sending out rays, rays of light,
          DI      CSI            DI        CSI
But never finding his way back home.

**(Bridge)**
     DI                   CSI
Oh, where are you in the dark?
DI   CSI        DI
O---------h, from shadows you call me
    BI
But I, I cannot see you!

**(Chorus)**

DI AI EI
Where is the love, where does it shine?
DI AI EI
I look at the world, and nothing I find!
DI AI EI
On a mountain I stand, calling your name,
DI AI EI
I reach out my hand, will you do the same?

Look at the rose, the flower of love,
With petals as soft as a lover's touch,
So warm and so sweet, you breathe in her scent,
Oh but make sure you don't breathe in too much,
For beneath the flowers lies the thorn,
Ready to tear your skin,
But the love it calls, and surrender you fall,
And the flower enfolds you within.

Me playing drums with Targa. Hungry Years Rock Club, Brighton, 1986

# Isís Unveiled

## (Damh the Bard)

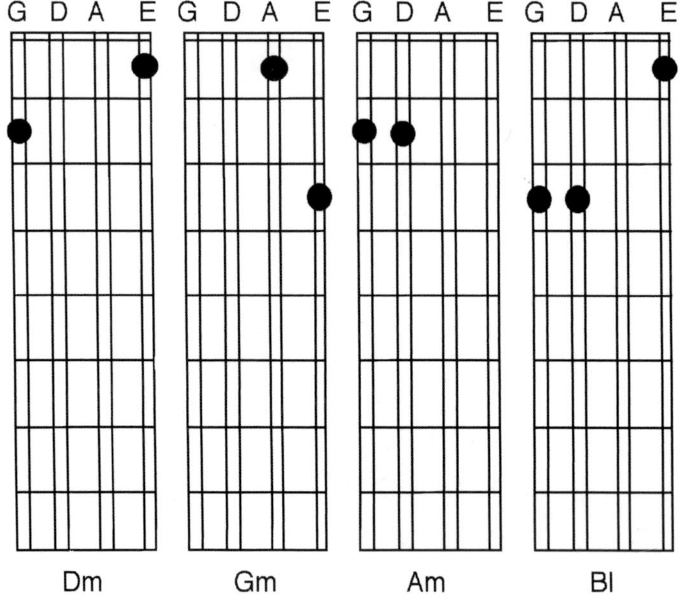

There was no denying it, for the first time in many years I was being visited by a Goddess from another land. Isis had always been a Goddess who had inspired me, but I had never written a song for her until this time. I had just bought a new mandola and was 'noodling' around with it, just playing around with notes, when this middle-eastern style riff came from out of nowhere. I continued playing, and it was like it had a life of its own, moving into a very nice key change - the Awen was flowing, and a song was on the way....

I put the mandolin down, and went to one of my altars to collect my figure of Isis - she is standing, one winged-arm outstretched, the other pointing to the ground. I placed her in on the table in front of me, and continued to play the tune. Before long the words were flowing, and her story was being told - from the game that formed her, to the reconstruction of Osiris, I saw a shadow formed by the light of the full moon, and within that shadow I watched as Set emerged from the darkness. I saw a coffin, floating down the nile, I saw her tears of joy falling onto the desert sand, bringing new life from the barren soil.

I was exhausted when it was done, but also very much at peace - a story told, a Goddess honoured.

Instrument: Mandola. Tuning: GDAE

Dm                                        Am
Play the game create the time,
                                    Dm
With every move and line,
                                        Am
Jackal God against the Moon,
                                            Gm
And the game will be over soon.
                                        Dm
Can you hear the Earth sighing?
                                        Gm
As he turns towards the sky,
                              Dm
The time of Ra is ending,
                                    BI
And the Sun begins to die.

**Chorus**

                                    Am
Can you feel it changing?
                                        BI
Can you see her in the night?
                                    Am
Can you feel it changing?

Sky and Earth they are as one,
Conceive daughter and sons,
Sister, lover, Goddess, Queen,
Mother to every living being,
Your light creates a shadow,
As you show your face unveiled,
Your brother Set betrays you,
There's a coffin on the Nile.

Fourteen pieces to the wind,
To all parts of the land,
Scattered widely she will find,
And make a lover from her hands,
The rain, her tears of gladness,
Fall to the fertile ground,
And Set caught in his madness,
To the desert he is bound.

# Morrighan
## (Damh the Bard)

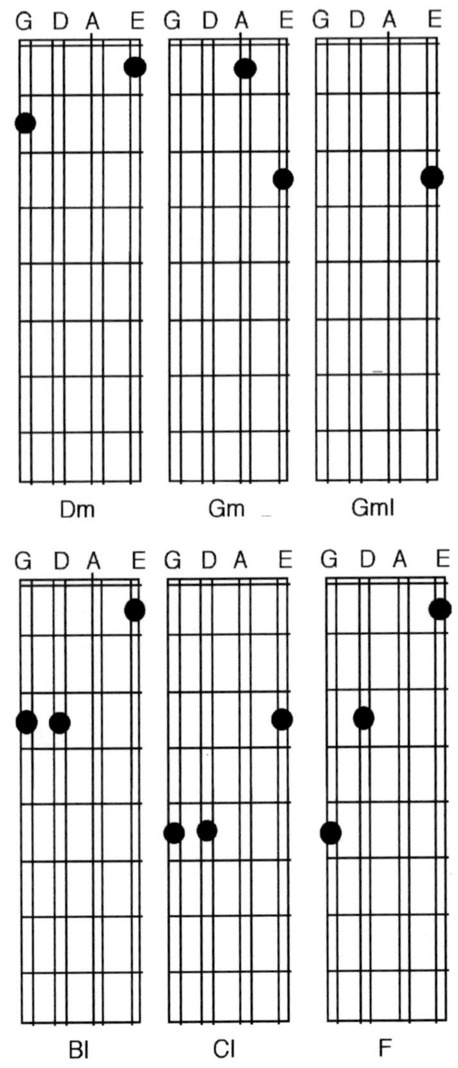

So there She is, looking at what we do to each other, in the name of religion, in the name of land, in the name of politics, and She shakes her head, not needing to take us yet, but we keep on coming, in ones, twos, and then by the thousand....

Instrument: Mandola. Tuning GDAE

```
Gm                GmI
Fingers of mist caress
   Gm                   GmI   Gm
Soldiers and fallen kings,
             GmI
A field lies silent
       Gm                         GmI
As an old crow spreads her wings
```

**(Chorus)**

```
              Dm
What do you see?
              Gm
What do you see?
           Dm          F
Cast your veil over the Sun.
     Gm
Morrighan
```

I have washed the blood away
And each will take your turn,
Another life given to me,
When will you ever learn?

**(Bridge 1)**

```
BI      CI      Gm                      BI          CI          Gm
                          And the will of man,
                    BI          CI          Gm
Lies heavy on the land,
                         BI          CI          Gm
Until you change your plan,
```

I'll be ready.

Night is falling,
But it's the noon of the day,
A flight of Ravens here,
To carry our souls away.

**(Bridge 2)**

I am the Phantom Queen,
And everything you've been,
And everything you've killed,
And all the blood you've spilled,
All the bullets and the guns,
All the Fathers and the Sons,
Lying dead in the streets,
Children crying at their feet,
Is this the world you want?
Look, the sun is fading away....

Damh is a modern-day Bard whose spirituality, and love of folk tradition, is expressed through his music, storytelling and poetry. Drawing on the Bardic traditions his performances are both entertaining and educational, weaving a tapestry of myth, peace, and anthems that speak directly to the heart, but never without a good splash of humour. Damh is a musical storyteller who works within the world of myth that cannot be proved; where the Faerie really do dance on Midsummer's Eve, where the trees talk, and the Hollow Hills take you into the realms of Annwn. Where the Goddess rides her horse, guiding you to magic, and the Horned God of old calls us from the shadows of the Greenwood.

This first volume contains chords and lyrics from Damh's first three albums:

Herne's Apprentice

Hills They Are Hollow

Spirit of Albion

Recordings of these songs are available on CD from:
www.BardicArts.com
Or if you are in the USA: www.cdbaby.com/all/damhbard
And also from iTunes as downloads

For further information: www.paganmusic.co.uk

Email: damh@paganmusic.co.uk

# FREE DETAILED CATALOGUE

Capall Bann is owned and run by people actively involved in many of the areas in which we publish. A detailed illustrated catalogue is available on request, SAE or International Postal Coupon appreciated. **Titles can be ordered direct from Capall Bann, post free in the UK** (cheque or PO with order) or from good bookshops and specialist outlets.

A Breath Behind Time, Terri Hector
A Soul is Born by Eleyna Williamson
Angels and Goddesses - Celtic Christianity & Paganism, M. Howard
The Art of Conversation With the Genius Loci, Barry Patterson
Arthur - The Legend Unveiled, C Johnson & E Lung
Astrology The Inner Eye - A Guide in Everyday Language, E Smith
Auguries and Omens - The Magical Lore of Birds, Yvonne Aburrow
Asyniur - Women's Mysteries in the Northern Tradition, S McGrath
Beginnings - Geomancy, Builder's Rites & Electional Astrology in the European Tradition, Nigel Pennick
Between Earth and Sky, Julia Day
The Book of Seidr, Runic John
Caer Sidhe - Celtic Astrology and Astronomy, Michael Bayley
Call of the Horned Piper, Nigel Jackson
Can't Sleep, Won't Sleep, Linda Louisa Dell
Carnival of the Animals, Gregor Lamb
Cat's Company, Ann Walker
Celebrating Nature, Gordon MacLellan
Celtic Faery Shamanism, Catrin James
Celtic Faery Shamanism - The Wisdom of the Otherworld, Catrin James
Celtic Lore & Druidic Ritual, Rhiannon Ryall
Celtic Sacrifice - Pre Christian Ritual & Religion, Marion Pearce
Celtic Saints and the Glastonbury Zodiac, Mary Caine
Circle and the Square, Jack Gale
Come Back To Life, Jenny Smedley
Company of Heaven, Jan McDonald
Compleat Vampyre - The Vampyre Shaman, Nigel Jackson
Cottage Witchcraft, Jan McDonald
Creating Form From the Mist - The Wisdom of Women in Celtic Myth and Culture, Lynne Sinclair-Wood
Crystal Clear - A Guide to Quartz Crystal, Jennifer Dent
Crystal Doorways, Simon & Sue Lilly

Crossing the Borderlines - Guising, Masking & Ritual Animal Disguise in the
European Tradition, Nigel Pennick
Dragons of the West, Nigel Pennick
Dreamtime by Linda Louisa Dell
Dreamweaver by Elen Sentier
Earth Dance - A Year of Pagan Rituals, Jan Brodie
Earth Harmony - Places of Power, Holiness & Healing, Nigel Pennick
Earth Magic, Margaret McArthur
Egyptian Animals - Guardians & Gateways of the Gods, Akkadia Ford
Eildon Tree (The) Romany Language & Lore, Michael Hoadley
Enchanted Forest - The Magical Lore of Trees, Yvonne Aburrow
Eternal Priestess, Sage Weston
Eternally Yours Faithfully, Roy Radford & Evelyn Gregory
Everything You Always Wanted To Know About Your Body, But So Far
Nobody's Been Able To Tell You, Chris Thomas & D Baker
Experiencing the Green Man, Rob Hardy & Teresa Moorey
Face of the Deep - Healing Body & Soul, Penny Allen
Fairies and Nature Spirits, Teresa Moorey
Fairies in the Irish Tradition, Molly Gowen
Familiars - Animal Powers of Britain, Anna Franklin
Flower Wisdom, Katherine Kear
Fool's First Steps, (The) Chris Thomas
Forest Paths - Tree Divination, Brian Harrison, Ill. S. Rouse
From Past to Future Life, Dr Roger Webber
From Stagecraft To Witchcraft, , Patricia Crowther
Gardening For Wildlife Ron Wilson
God Year, The, Nigel Pennick & Helen Field
Goddess on the Cross, Dr George Young
Goddess Year, The, Nigel Pennick & Helen Field
Goddesses, Guardians & Groves, Jack Gale
Handbook For Pagan Healers, Liz Joan
Handbook of Fairies, Ronan Coghlan
Healing Book, The, Chris Thomas and Diane Baker
Healing Homes, Jennifer Dent
Healing Journeys, Paul Williamson
Healing Stones, Sue Philips
Heathen Paths - Viking and Anglo Saxon Beliefs by Pete Jennings
Herb Craft - Shamanic & Ritual Use of Herbs, Lavender & Franklin
Hidden Heritage - Exploring Ancient Essex, Terry Johnson
Hub of the Wheel, Skytoucher
In and Out the Windows, Dilys Gator
In Search of Herne the Hunter, Eric Fitch
In Search of the Green Man, Peter Hill
Inner Celtia, Alan Richardson & David Annwn
Inner Mysteries of the Goths, Nigel Pennick
Inner Space Workbook - Develop Through Tarot, Cat Summers & Julian Vayne

In Search of Pagan Gods, Teresa Moorey
Intuitive Journey, Ann Walker Isis - African Queen, Akkadia Ford
Journey Home, The, Chris Thomas
Kecks, Keddles & Kesh - Celtic Lang & The Cog Almanac, Bayley
Language of the Psycards, Berenice
Legend of Robin Hood, The, Richard Rutherford-Moore
Lid Off the Cauldron, Patricia Crowther
Light From the Shadows - Modern Traditional Witchcraft, Gwyn
Living Tarot, Ann Walker
Lore of the Sacred Horse, Marion Davies
Lost Lands & Sunken Cities (2nd ed.), Nigel Pennick
Lyblác, Anglo Saxon Witchcraft by Wulfeage
The Magic and Mystery of Trees, Teresa Moorey
Magic For the Next 1,000 Years, Jack Gale
Magic of Herbs - A Complete Home Herbal, Rhiannon Ryall
Magical Guardians - Exploring the Spirit and Nature of Trees, Philip Heselton
Magical History of the Horse, Janet Farrar & Virginia Russell
Magical Lore of Animals, Yvonne Aburrow
Magical Lore of Cats, Marion Davies
Magical Lore of Herbs, Marion Davies
Magick Without Peers, Ariadne Rainbird & David Rankine
Masks of Misrule - Horned God & His Cult in Europe, Nigel Jackson
Medicine For The Coming Age, Lisa Sand MD
Medium Rare - Reminiscences of a Clairvoyant, Muriel Renard
Menopausal Woman on the Run, Jaki da Costa
Mind Massage - 60 Creative Visualisations, Marlene Maundrill
Mirrors of Magic - Evoking the Spirit of the Dewponds, P Heselton
The Moon and You, Teresa Moorey
Moon Mysteries, Jan Brodie
Mysteries of the Runes, Michael Howard
Mystic Life of Animals, Ann Walker
New Celtic Oracle The, Nigel Pennick & Nigel Jackson
Oracle of Geomancy, Nigel Pennick
Pagan Feasts - Seasonal Food for the 8 Festivals, Franklin & Phillips
Paganism For Teens, Jess Wynne
Patchwork of Magic - Living in a Pagan World, Julia Day
Pathworking - A Practical Book of Guided Meditations, Pete Jennings
Personal Power, Anna Franklin
Pickingill Papers - The Origins of Gardnerian Wicca, Bill Liddell
Pillars of Tubal Cain, Nigel Jackson
Places of Pilgrimage and Healing, Adrian Cooper
Planet Earth - The Universe's Experiment, Chris Thomas
Practical Divining, Richard Foord
Practical Meditation, Steve Hounsome
Practical Spirituality, Steve Hounsome
Psychic Self Defence - Real Solutions, Jan Brodie

Real Fairies, David Tame
Reality - How It Works & Why It Mostly Doesn't, Rik Dent
Romany Tapestry, Michael Houghton
Runic Astrology, Nigel Pennick
Sacred Animals, Gordon MacLellan
Sacred Celtic Animals, Marion Davies, Ill. Simon Rouse
Sacred Dorset - On the Path of the Dragon, Peter Knight
Sacred Grove - The Mysteries of the Forest, Yvonne Aburrow
Sacred Geometry, Nigel Pennick
Sacred Nature, Ancient Wisdom & Modern Meanings, A Cooper
Sacred Ring - Pagan Origins of British Folk Festivals, M. Howard
Season of Sorcery - On Becoming a Wisewoman, Poppy Palin
Seasonal Magic - Diary of a Village Witch, Paddy Slade
Secret Places of the Goddess, Philip Heselton
Secret Signs & Sigils, Nigel Pennick
The Secrets of East Anglian Magic, Nigel Pennick
A Seeker's Guide To Past Lives, Paul Williamson
Seeking Pagan Gods, Teresa Moorey
A Seer's Guide To Crystal Divination, Gale Halloran
Self Enlightenment, Mayan O'Brien
Soul Resurgence, Poppy Palin
Spirits of the Air, Jaq D Hawkins
Spirits of the Water, Jaq D Hawkins
Spirits of the Fire, Jaq D Hawkins
Spirits of the Aether, Jaq D Hawkins
Spirits of the Earth, Jaq D Hawkins
Stony Gaze, Investigating Celtic Heads John Billingsley
Stumbling Through the Undergrowth , Mark Kirwan-Heyhoe
Subterranean Kingdom, The, revised 2nd ed, Nigel Pennick
Symbols of Ancient Gods, Rhiannon Ryall
Talking to the Earth, Gordon MacLellan
Talking With Nature, Julie Hood
Taming the Wolf - Full Moon Meditations, Steve Hounsome
Teachings of the Wisewomen, Rhiannon Ryall
The Other Kingdoms Speak, Helena Hawley
Transformation of Housework, Ben Bushill
Tree: Essence of Healing, Simon & Sue Lilly
Tree: Essence, Spirit & Teacher, Simon & Sue Lilly
Tree Seer, Simon & Sue Lilly
Torch and the Spear, Patrick Regan
Understanding Chaos Magic, Jaq D Hawkins
Understanding Past Lives, Dilys Gater
Understanding Second Sight, Dilys Gater
Understanding Spirit Guides, Dilys Gater
Understanding Star Children, Dilys Gater
The Urban Shaman, Dilys Gater

Vortex - The End of History, Mary Russell
Warp and Weft - In Search of the I-Ching, William de Fancourt
Warriors at the Edge of Time, Jan Fry
Water Witches, Tony Steele
Way of the Magus, Michael Howard
Weaving a Web of Magic, Rhiannon Ryall
West Country Wicca, Rhiannon Ryall
What's Your Poison? vol 1, Tina Tarrant
Wheel of the Year, Teresa Moorey & Jane Brideson
Wildwitch - The Craft of the Natural Psychic, Poppy Palin
Wildwood King , Philip Kane
A Wisewoman's Book of Tea Leaf Reading, Pat Barki
The Witching Path, Moira Stirland
The Witch's Kitchen, Val Thomas
The Witches' Heart, Eileen Smith
Treading the Mill - Practical CraftWorking in Modern Traditional Witchcraft by Nigel Pearson
Witches of Oz, Matthew & Julia Philips
Witchcraft Myth Magic Mystery and... Not Forgetting Fairies, Ralph Harvey
Wondrous Land - The Faery Faith of Ireland by Dr Kay Mullin
Working With Crystals, Shirley o'Donoghue
Working With Natural Energy, Shirley o'Donoghue
Working With the Merlin, Geoff Hughes
Your Talking Pet, Ann Walker
The Zodiac Experience, Patricia Crowther

# FREE detailed catalogue and FREE 'Inspiration' magazine

## Contact: Capall Bann Publishing, Auton Farm, Milverton, Somerset, TA4 1NE